Ancient Ephesus and Earliest Christianity: Culture, Architecture and St Paul

Deslee Campbell

---

1.   http://www.zondedrvan.com/

The photograph of the Grand Theatre of Ephesus, used on the front cover, is by QuartierLatin, 1968, and is used under the terms of flickr Creative Commons Attribution Share Alike 2.0 Licenses.

Table of Contents

Chapter 1
Social, Political and Commercial Environment

1.1. The site

Ephesus in an ancient city of the West coast of modern Turkey and the Greek Island of Patmos is not far away in the Aegean Sea. Settlement near the present site of Ephesus can now be date to Neolithic times but it was hardly a city. It was said to have been founded by the mythical hero Androcles in their equivalent of the Dream Time but after the death of the Macedonian conqueror, Alexander the Great, in 323 B.C. this early city was replaced by the site currently known as Ancient Ephesus.

It was selected by the general Lysimachos to replace the original site and Lysimachos removed the people from one site to the other. He also imported people from other places to increase the population so that Anatolia's largest city was created. During the time of the Emperor Augustus (43 B.C-14 A.D.) it was made the capital of the Roman Province of Asia.

The topography (the harbour, the hills and the river valley) determined the city-plan in the Greek manner. It was not a planned Roman city with the usual Cardo Maximus and Decumanis Maximus crossing each other at right angles and there was no overarching grid pattern in the street-layout. In fact the main thoroughfare wound its way along the narrow stretches of low land between Mt Pion to the North-East and Mt Koressos in the South-West. Elevated land rises up on every side, close to the buildings, especially in the South, and the Grand Theatre, the Odeion and the homes of the wealthy, on the South of the Curetes Street, utilise the landforms by being built into hillsides. In the Northern distance Mt Ayasoluk overlooks the city.

Map 1A. Map of Greece, the Asian coast and the Aegean Sea.
Key: A=Athens, B=Beroea, C=Corinth, D=Derbe, E=Ehpesus, H=Hierapolis, I=Iconium, J=Jerusalem, L= Laodicaea, M=Miletus, N=Neapolis, P=Philippi, R=Rhodes, S.A.= Syrian Antioch, T=Troas in Turkey and Thessalonika in Ancient Macedonia (now Salonica in Greece).

1.2. Early History

Ephesus began life as a Greek-Macedonian colony but was absorbed into the Roman Empire in 139 B.C. It was briefly controlled by the king of Pergamon/Pergamum but came back under Roman rule in 6 B.C. and paid heavy taxes to Rome. In return Rome built a system of underground clay pipes to distribute water throughout the city: to fountains, baths, latrines and the homes of the wealthy elite. Roman influence can be detected in the inscriptions on the monuments which were generally in Greek but in the Pauline Period some were in both Greek and Latin.

From the reign of the Emperor Augustus (43 B.C-14 A.D.) and for two hundred years Ephesus experienced a golden age in which the city controlled the banking affairs of the region and was a provincial capital city and seat of government.[1] The number of monumental buildings devoted to leisure pursuits attests to the wealth of the population, notably the Stadium, the Grand Theatre and the numerous gymnasia. The terraced sector in the centre of town, which contained seven homes of the wealthy elite, confirm this conclusion as some even had more than a dozen rooms and internal plumbing for a fountain, a bathroom and latrines.

Two very serious earthquakes did much damage to Ephesus, first in 23 A.D and again in 275 A.D. Many structures, indeed much of the city, required rebuilding and repairs.

1.3. Ephesus: A Great Port City

The city's location on a safe harbour site enhanced its prosperity even though the silting up of the harbour was a constant problem requiring dredging. Even though large ships could not navigate the harbour it was still a busy port. Ephesus is positioned near many of the Aegean Islands not just Patmos, and the large island of Crete and Rhodes are not far away. From Ephesus, ships could esasily cross the Aegean to the great trading cities of Athens and Corinth. Ehpesus was also a clearing house for merchandise coming from the vast hinterland through Turkey, Russia and as far as China on its way to Egypt, Rome and Greece. As will be shown, passengers and pilgrims also greatly enhanced the city's prosperity.

1.3. In the 1st Century

After his conversion to Christianity in about 34-36 A.D., St Paul (c.5 A.D. - c.67/68 A.D.) ministered in Asia Minor and around the Aegean Sea. Paul's travels included to Ephesus where the Christian message may well have already taken root. When St Paul arrived, St John the Apostle may have already settled there, in which case there was already a Johannine congregation,[2] although some think St John came in his older age, after Jerusalem was destroyed in 70 A.D. It was St Paul, however, who made the early dramatic impact, which St Luke recorded for posterity. Paul came at a key time, before the cult of emperor worship became established, after which it would have been harder and more dangerous to make inroads against the cult of imperial power. There were, however, many established cults, which dominated Ephesian social and political life.

Ephesus was a grand, cosmopolitan and famous city. Silt brought downstream by the Cayster River was already beginning to silt up the river to the North and the harbour to the West of the city but in the mid-1st-century Ephesus was still a thriving port-city. It had an artificial harbour that needed to be constantly dredged and the largest ships could not navigate its waters. There was much building activity during St Paul's lifetime although the essentials had already been built, as will be detailed below.

1.4. Imperial Constructions

Various Roman emperors, both before and after the Pauline Period, played an important role in embellishing the city (and their own reputations in the process). These imperial endowments provided work for architects, quarry workers, stonemasons, builders, painters, mosaicists, artists, unskilled labourers and support staff. Stone carvers and builders in stone were essential because locally sourced marble was usually used and everything was intricately carved: not just statues, busts, human heads and animal figures but trellis and lattice work, finials, corbels, garlands and capitals. Mosaics were also created, for out-door areas as well as homes and buildings. The work was almost constant, noisy and dusty.

During the reign of the Emperor Augustus at the turn of the eras important structures had been built such as the twin temples of Bona Dea and Julius Caesar, a temple to Augustus himself, the State Agora and its Basilica and the government palace or Prytaneion (although its eternal flame was much older). Some emperors, such as Augustus, visited Ephesus: and Hadrian visited three times. Imperial consent had to be obtained for major constructions, especially temples.

Important structures were erected during these periods: Augustus (43 B.C.-14 A.D.): Temples; Basilica; Triumphal Arch; Prytaneion

Claudius (41-54 A.D.): theatre; Fountain House; paving of Harbour Street

Nero (54-68 A.D.): Stadium; Basilica; Fountain, repairs to, and the *socle* of Marble Rd.

Domitian (81-96 A.D.): his Temple built and Domitian Square laid out.

Trajan (96-117 A.D.): a fountain with his great statue.

Hadrian (117-148 A.D.): small temple; Gate (Triumphal Arch); Olympeum.[3]

Antoninus Pius (138-161): completed Hadrian's works; Vedius Baths.

Marcus Aurelius (151-169): the Great Antonine Altar Constantius (317-361): Harbour Baths renovated.

Arcadius (395-408): rebuilt Harbour Road and its environs

1.5. Construction Work in the Pauline Period (c.34-68 A.D.)

Much building activity was taking place during the Pauline Period and would have been seen during Paul's extensive visits there. Under the Emperor Claudius (41-54 A.D.) the Grand Theatre was being enlarged and a Fountain House with Ionic columns was built beside it to supply clean water to theatre-patrons (Plate 4.3b). When Harbour Road was paved from the Grand Theatre down to the harbour, and because the Fountain House gave them water, people began to settle down Harbour Road and to the North, around the Stadium, which was near the Koressos Gate in the Northern City Wall. The Harbour Baths, the largest in Ephesus, and perhaps the oldest, were not far away (marked on Map 4A).

After 54 A.D., under the Emperor Nero (54-68 A.D.) the Stadium (or Circus) was renovated,4 the backdrop (s *kene*) of the Great Theatre was built, a large room was added to the Basilica in the State Agora and a covered portico or elevated walkway (a *socle*) was built to keep pedestrians off Marble Road, which was reserved for vehicles (Plate 4.4).

1.6. The State Agora and Government buildings of Ephesus

As shown in Map 1B, the administration of the city was centred in a particular quarter of Ephesus, the prime position. The quarter probably dated back to the death of Alexander the Great when the city was established on this site. The area was progressively added to even up to the Byzantine (Christian) period, for example by the Temple of Domitian (81-96 A.D.) and a square to enhance it, and the fountain built by the proconsul (governor), Laecanius Bassus, in A.D. 80, and a church dedicated to the Virgin Mary (1st-half-2nd-century)[5].

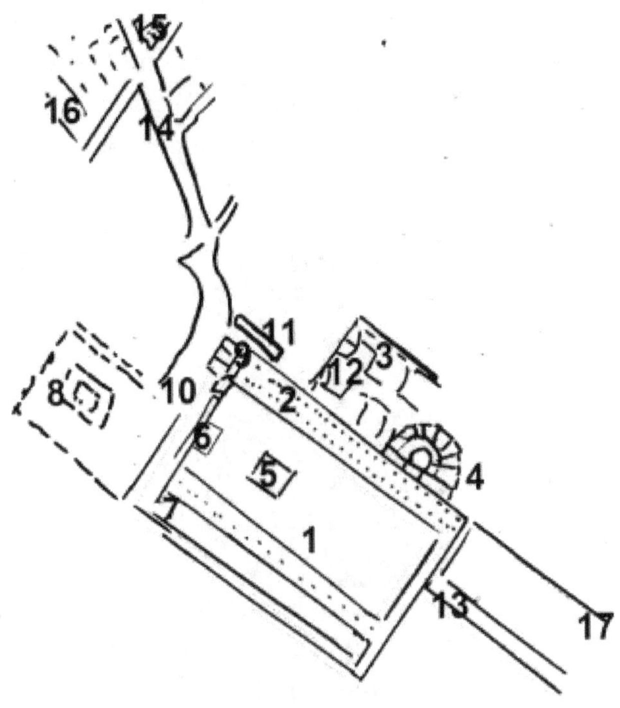

Map 1B. Key: 1=State Agora, 2=Basilica, 3=Prytaneion, 4=The Odeion, 5=Isis Temple, 6=Pollio Fountain, 7=Bassus Fountain, 8=Temple of Domitian, 9=Temple of Augustus, 10=Domitian Square, 11=Memmius Monument, 12=Twin Temples, 13=Sacred Way, 14=Curetes Street, 15=Scholastikia Baths, 16=Terrace Houses, 17=Baths/Gymnasium.

In the Pauline Period the government-and-administration area consisted of these elements: the large State Agora with its basilica; the Stoas of the State Agora; the Prytaneion (or government palace), the twin temples of Bona Dea and Julius Caesar, the Temple of Augustus, the Pollio Fountain and perhaps a precursor to the Odeion as a temporary meeting place for town councillors. These elements will be detailed in Chapter 4, below.

1.7. Construction Work After the Pauline Period After the Pauline Period, apart from the Odeion, construction work mainly consisted of either repairs and enlargements, or gifts from emperors and wealthy citizens that were of a decorative nature; 6

Plate 1.1. Trajan's fountain today. [6]

Plate 1.2. Hadrian's Temple. Public domain.[8]

[See Appendix 1 for his patronage.] [7]

embellishments to the city rather than essentials. For example, a temple was built to the Emperor Domitian (81-96 A.D.) and a wealthy citizen, Tiberius Claudius Aristion, built a once-magnificent fountain for the Emperor Trajan (98-117 A.D.) which featured his huge statue. Only Trajan's foot standing upon the orb of the Earth remains and it is under the arch (Plate 1.1). The current state of the building does no justice to the original.

Nearby, an admirer built Hadrian (117-138 A.D.) an attractive but small temple or monument, with his huge statue within the *cella*, inside (Plate 1.2). He, himself, built a temple to Zeus north of the Grand Theatre.

These monuments made Ephesus even grander and helped the city vie with other cities to earn the title 'temple-guardian' which Ephesus was granted four times, although Ephesus already housed one of the Seven Wonders of the Ancient World, the Artemision or Temple of Artemis.

The Roman goddess Diana was called Artemis by the local Greek-speaking people and, in Ephesus, she was mainly depicted as a multi-breasted fertility goddess; but also as a scantily-clad huntress with a bow and arrow or spear.

1.8. Religious Cults

Many provincial notables lived in Ephesus because it was the chief city of the Roman Province of Asia and the centre of the cult of the Roman goddess Diana (Artemis). People travelled from near and far to visit her huge all-marble temple, which is detailed in Chapter 2. They brought gifts, made sacrifices and paid homage to her huge multi-breasted statue there and in the markets they purchased small silver, copper or bronze copies of her temple and her image to take home with them. Over 100 examples of Artemis have been found.[9]

Magic sorcery and secret cults Magic, sorcery and secret cults were also strong in Ephesus and deceased ancestors were worshipped, especially in February during the Parentilia festival.[10] Many deities,

Greek, Roman, Anatolian and Egyptian, were worshipped in homes, cult centres, temples and during festivals and sporting contests in Ephesus. Androklos/Androcles, the mythical founder of Ephesus, was worshipped. The Egyptian gods, Isis and Serapis, at one time had their own substantial temple there.[11]

In the mid 1st century, at least fourteen deities were worshipped in Ephesus[12] many of the female deities, including: Artemis/Diana, Roma, Niki (winged Victory), Aphrodite, Athena, Demeter, Ge, Isis, Hestia, Cybele and Bona Dea (the Good Goddess). One myth-of-origin held that Ephesus had been founded by a race of warrior women (Amazons) and women were more forward in civil and cultic life than was usual for the era. This formed a back-story to some of St Paul's teachings.

When the Grand Theatre was used in the Pauline Period all actors were male and they all wore masks to designate their characters. Before performances began a ceremony in honour of Dionysus (Bacchus), the god of wine, would take place before the altar.[13]

There are over 1,000 published inscriptions from Ephesus and many of them concern deities.[14] The attire of the Great Statue of Artemis in her temple featured images of the signs of the Zodiac[15] and she was invoked in spells.[16] This is typical of syncretism and the melding of beliefs. Although there is evidence of magic melded in some way with Judaism,[17] ideally it and Christianity remained aloof, although in the early Pauline Period Christianity and Judaism were rarely distinguished. Because St Paul preached in synagogues as much as possible he would have been seen by casual observers as a Jew (which, of course, he was).

Visitors brought wealth to the city and employment was provided for the priests and priestesses of the Artemis cult and those of other deities whose cults also flourished. In fact religion was central to the survival of the city. It would soon also become a centre for the cult of emperor-worship, after monuments, such as fountains, temples and huge statues, were constructed by or for the Emperors Augustus, Domitian (later rededicated to his father), Trajan and Hadrian and an altar to or for Antoninous Pius. There was even a small temple for the deified Julius Caesar, although he had not officially been an emperor.

The Pauline period was early days for emperor-worship as the Roman Empire, as distinct from the Roman Republic, only began with Augustus (43 B.C.-14 A.D.) so the imperial cult developed and expanded alongside and in competition with Christianity.[18] Augustus was deified after his death but later emperors, such as Domitian and Hadrian, would not wait to die before expecting worship. Eventually Ephesus would have three or four official temples for the Imperial Cult, which meant that it was awarded the honour of 'temple warden' (*neokoros*) for each one; as well as also earning the title for the great Temple of Artemis.[19]

1.9. Economic Prosperity

Much wealth also came to Ephesus from trade through its safe harbour at the mouth of the Cayster River, which is where its earliest buildings were to be found. Ephesus was the end-point of great caravan routes. A vast hinterland, stretching back to the Euphrates River and beyond, fed goods into Ephesus on their way to Greece, Italy, Egypt and the many Aegean Islands. Such trade also involved imported goods, with the Ephesian merchants being the middle-men. The city also had an industrial area where metal products, wine and perfumes were produced and also a mint, because the city was permitted to strike its own gold and silver coins.[20] The harbour was very busy, employing hundreds of workers. Wealth also came from land: vast estates that grew wheat, barley, citrus, grapes, olives, vegetables and tobacco.[21]

Land could be owned by wealthy women, independently. They could own vineyards but were not normally permitted to drink the produce.

Apart from priests/priestesses, temple prostitutes, politicians, councillors or merchants, the following occupations were pursued in 1st-century Ephesus: sailor, doctor, builder, quarry worker, carpenter, stone carver, wood cutter, knob turner, jeweller, silversmith, coppersmith, metal worker, cobbler, hemp worker, wool dealer, garment dealer, dyer, baker, teacher, gym instructor, public servant, transport worker, carter, worker in the baths, midwife, wet-nurse and slave. There may also have been street-vendors. As there were two lakes nearby, seafood was caught and processed from the lakes and the ocean. Ephesus was also known for schools that taught painting, sculpture, teaching and medicine.

1.10. Conclusions

When St Paul arrived in Ephesus in the mid-1st century A.D. it was a large, important, prosperous, cosmopolitan, busy but peaceful city with a special devotion to Artemis and other, mainly female, deities. Many of the buildings for which it became famous had not yet been built but the overall layout and the essentials were in place and construction work was proceeding.

Chapter 2
The Cult of Artemis and the Artemision

2.1. Artemis (Diana of the Ephesians)

In 1st-century Ephesus the most important deity was Artemis who was equivalent to the Roman goddess, Diana. She became the goddess of both nature and fertility, and *"was served by a host of prostitutes"*[22] both male and female.[23]

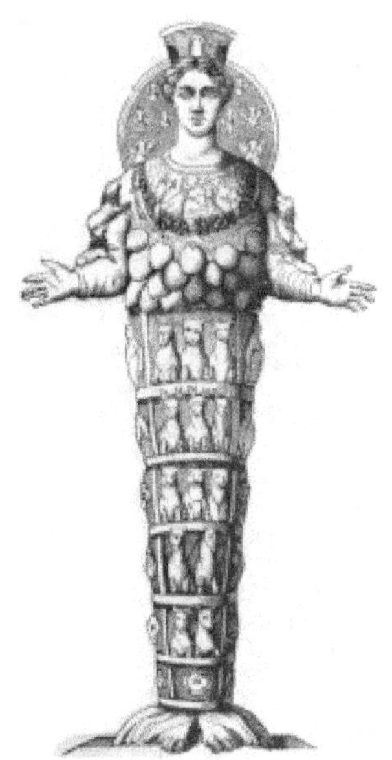

Plate 2.1. Drawing of a version of Artemis. Public domain.

Diana had two personas and was depicted quite differently in each. As 'Diana the huntress' Artemis was depicted scantily clad, carrying a bow and arrow and accompanied by a deer. As 'Artemis of Ephesus' she was depicted wearing an elaborate headdress and a long concealing garment, but with multiple egg-like objects on her torso (Plate 2.1). Whether these were breasts, eggs or bulls testicles is debated but they signified fertility.[24] The belief was that the statue of the deity, unlike a painting, was not a representation of the god or goddess but **was** the deity, and could, therefore, perform miracles, bring healings, prophesies, dreams and respond to petitions. She was the guardian of the city, of virgins and (strangely) also of childbirth.[25]

2.2. Cybele and Artemis

In Asia Minor a major local cult had been of Cybele, the mother goddess of fertility, motherhood and the mountain-wilds in Asia Minor, a cult that had already merged with the identity of Astarte and Ishtar. Greek colonists introduced Artemis to Asia and she was readily accepted.[26] Some scholars opine that Cybele's identity was combined with that of the Roman goddess Diana[27] but other scholars contest this conclusion in favour of the two goddesses retaining their separate identities.[28]

The cult of Cybele (Mother of the Gods) was excluded from Rome for a long time because its orgies were unsavoury and Romans found castration abhorrent. Male priests, called *Galli/Gallai*, castrated themselves and lacerated their bodies with knives in a noisy frenzy of pain and gore. This was done in memory of Attis who had promised to love Cybele in spiritual devotion but betrayed his love by marrying a nymph. Cybele extracted revenge by driving him mad so that he castrated himself in self-punishment, before dying. The Emperor known as Julian the Apostate (361-363) was initiated into the mysteries of Cybele in caverns in Ephesus, and, in Athens, both he and, earlier, the Emperor Hadrian were initiated into the secretive Eleusian

Mysteries of the goddesses Demeter and her daughter Persephone (A.K.A. Kore), in Athens.[29]

Women used wine and blood sacrifices in Cybele's rituals, which were otherwise forbidden to them. It was believed that Dionysus, the god of wine, had been taught the rites that pertained to his cult by Cybele and *"these rites were closely akin to one another"*.[30]

2.3. The Temple of Artemis in Ephesus

The Artemision, or Temple of Artemis in Ephesus, was the first ancient building constructed entirely of marble and was declared to be one of the Seven Wonders of the Ancient World by the poet Antipater of Solon in c. 140 A.D. He said that, apart from Olympus, the sun never shone on anything as grand as this temple. A copy has been constructed in Istanbul (Plate 2.3).

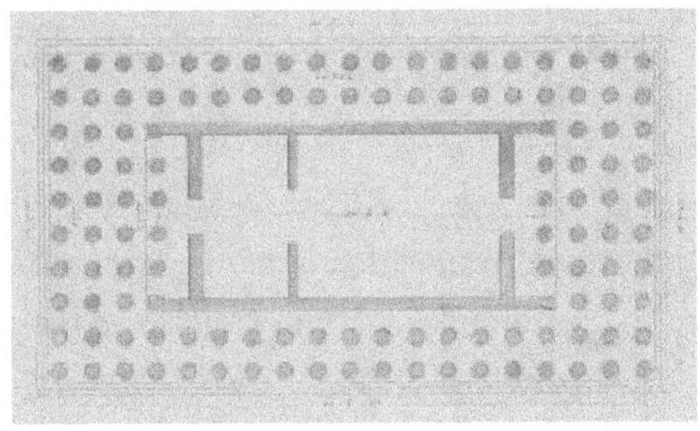

Plate 2.2. The Later Temple of Artemis. Public domain.

In its first phase (c.1100 BC), this sacred site consisted of just an altar, but recently cult objects have been found in an even lower stratum, dated 6th century B.C. In about 560 B.C. a temple was built over the remains of the altar and it lasted about 200 years but, in 323 or

365 B.C., it was deliberately burnt down. The Ephesians rebuilt it to exactly the same plan but upon a 3 metre high pedestal because the selected site was marshy ground, which supposedly would withstand earthquakes.[31] Now, only one column of the Artemision is left standing.[32]

The sacred inner portion of the Artemision was rectangular with its main elements being a semi-external porch and a sanctuary of two parts. This was surrounded by a forest of fluted Greek columns of the Ionic order, including columns inside the porch. The interior of the Artemision was unroofed but the statue of the goddess had a protective canopy or baldachin over it. Being one of the Seven Wonders of the Ancient World this temple was the pride of the city, admired near and far. It was this replacement temple which stood during the 1st century. It appears that only men, virgins and slave women were permitted near the Artemision, while other women would be put to death.[33] The annual festival of Artemis lasted one month and offerings of one month's salary were given, which is why priests were among the very wealthy.[34]

Married women were not entirely excluded from cultic life as the annual Thesmophoria festival, which lasted three days and two nights, was reserved for them, moreover the cult rituals and the secret name of Bona Dea was known only by women.

Although St Paul may not have visited the glittering, white temple it would have been seen in the distance when he stayed in Ephesus for about three years, but its influence upon the city could not be ignored. Nor could St Paul's preaching be ignored by those whose livelihoods depended upon the popularity of the cult of Artemis. This is illustrated in Plate 2.3. When people who had practised sorcery converted to Christianity they brought their magical texts to St Paul and publicly burned them (Acts 19:18-20).

On one occasion metalworkers and craftsmen, followers of her cult who made money by selling shrines of Artemis, led by Demetrius the silversmith, caused a riot against St Paul. They shouted in the theatre and the streets and chanted, *Great is Artemis of the Ephesians*" (Acts 19:21-41 and 20:1). In the Grand Theatre, the town clerk (a well-known top official who was like the mayor) was able to quell the riot against St Paul. Provincial religious leaders (Asiarchs) sent Paul a message not to enter the Theatre. Their concern for Paul's welfare suggests that Christianity was reaching the highest levels of power. Regard for the safety of his co-workers forced Paul to leave town very soon.

Plate 2.3. St Paul preaching against magic in Ephesus.[35]

When St Paul sailed past this coastline again he asked the leaders of the Ephesian church to come to meet him at Miletus, perhaps to prevent further trouble in the city (Acts 20:16-17) although it is highly probable that he returned to Ephesus a few years later, after his first imprisonment.

2.4. The Importance of the Artemision to Ephesus

It is difficult to understand just how entrenched the religious cults that prevailed in Antiquity were, pervading every aspect of social, political and family life. Even lighting a fire for cooking involved taking a flame from the sacred, eternal fire that burned at the Temple of Hestia.

Usually, in Antiquity, a new cult had to syncretised with the established religion, just as the worship of Cybele had melded with that of other female deities. Christianity, like Judaism, could not, and would not, accommodate such syncretism and required a complete break with past practices, including altering their former clothing and hairstyles.

This was evidenced in Ephesus when converts brought their books of magic to St Paul and publicly burned them (Acts 19:19) (Plate 2.3) but Paul's congregation was perhaps 500 people out of a total population of between 20,000 and 25,000. [36]

Among the regular celebrations held in the city were festive processions from the Artemision on a route that was called 'the Processional Way'. This wound its way from the Temple, through the city via the eastern gate,[37] onto the Ceretes Street and Marble Road, past the Grand Theatre to the Koressos Gate beside the Stadium before returning to the Artemision (Map 5A). These events would have attracted pilgrims, promoted commerce and enhanced the status of the city.

In 1905, under the original altar to Artemis, archaeologists discovered a hoard of the oldest Greek coins. They had been minted in Ephesus, Miletus and other cities nearby.[38] The Temple of Artemis functioned as a repository for the money and valuables from neighbouring cities and so built up a reputation for managing money, and for business.

Plate 2.4. Temple of Artemis, model in Istanbul. [39]
Photograph: Ze Prime, 2007.37

2.5. Conclusions

Artemis worship with making money, or separately, were key forces at work in ancient Ephesian society, and magic was very strong. Even though the worship of Artemis was entrenched, St Paul, with his teaching of 'the way', made such progress in Ephesus that he was violently opposed. This was because his teachings reduced the income of those who made a living out of the cult and because it offended the great goddess in person.

Chapter 3

The City in the 1st Century

3.1. What Ephesus was like in the mid-1st century A.D.

When the apostle first visited, the essentials of the city that stretched back to the founding of the city by Lysimachos after the death of Alexander the Great, had been set in place. The city was not as grand as it became later and many of the favourite sites that tourists see now did not yet exist. The Celsus Library, the Odeion and the Temple of Hadrian had not been built and the Marble Road was not yet been upgraded and paved with marble.

3.2. St Paul would have seen or known the following completed buildings and works-in-progress

The essentials of the city, 'the nuts and bolts', were in place by the time St Paul arrived, but the city was less monumental and simpler than it later became but, nevertheless, Ephesus was a well-established and well-endowed city, as these 32 examples indicate.

Finished Work by Paul's or Nero's death (68 A.D)

1. City walls (10m high by 9km long) and its gates.

2. Harbour Gateway (propylon)

3. Harbour Baths and gymnasium (Plate 4.1).

4. The Temple of Artemis (the Artemision) (Plate 2.3).

5. A Nymphaeum from the 1st century B.C.

6. Sacred Way to the Artemesion (Plate 5.5).

7. Streets and their columns.

8. Sewerage lines that ran beneath the paving stones.

9. Roman Aqueduct.

10. The Marnas Aqueduct and its fountain South of the State Agora.

11. The Bassus Water Palace (a large water-storage cistern).

12. A Hellenistic-period fountain of the 3rd to 2nd century B.C.

13. Marble latrines with mosaic floors and running water (Plate 5.8).

14. Brothels and baths.

15. The Grand Theatre (Plate 4.3a).

16. The *Heroon* (mausoleum) of Androclus, 'founder' of the city.

17. The mausoleum of Arisone IV, half-sister of Cleopatra.

18. A Fountain House beside the Theatre (Plate 4.3b).

19. The State Agora with the merchant's Basilica (Plate 5.1).

20. The Lower Agora (Commercial Agora) (Plate 4.5).

21. The Mazaeus-Mithridates Gate (Plate 4.6).

22. Pedestrian colonnade or *scole* beside 'Marble Road' (Plate 4.4).

23. Shops that lined the main street (Plate 6.1a).

24. Municipal Palace (Prytaneion) with a perpetual flame (Plate 5.2).

25. Houses of the wealthy or middle-class people (Plates 6.1b, 6.2).

26. Harbour Road (Plate 6.1).

27. The Arch of Triumph (built in 3 B.C., the time of Augustus).

28. Temple of Augustus beside the State Agora, a Sebasteion.

29. Dwellings for ordinary people.

30. The monument of the Memmius family (Plate 5.6).

31. The lecture hall of Tyrannus.

32. The synagogue or synagogues.

Monuments under construction during St Paul's lifetime:

1. Embellishments to the market place (Commercial Agora)

2. More houses of the wealthy built.

3. Enlargement of the Grand Theatre.

4. A room added to the Basilica in the State Agora by Nero.

5. Rebuilding of the Stadium by Nero (54-68 A.D.).

3.3. The Stadium or Circus

The Stadium, which was on the North edge of the city, was built in the 1st century B.C. and remodelled by the Emperor Nero (54-68 A.D.). Gladiatorial fighting against men and wild beasts began first in Ephesus, from about 70 B.C., with as many as twenty-five imported African animals being killed during five-day festivals.[40] A whole industry grew up around fights and festivals of combat and slaughter, including the training of gladiators.[41] *"Gladiatorial combats and wild animal contests, feasts and processions were an important part of imperial cult celebrations".*[42] Local wildlife was also hunted for sport. St Paul was well aware of this cultural element and compared his work with that of a gladiator (II Tim. 4:7) but he did not condemn these events. By modern standards life in Ephesus was tough, brutal, bloodthirsty and governed by superstitions.

3.4. The Harbour Baths and Gymnasium

The huge Harbour Baths and its gymnasium were the largest and perhaps the oldest: rebuilt under the Emperor Domitian (81-96 A.D.) and, thirty or so years later, renovated, embellished and enlarged at great expense by the chief priest of Asia, Claudius Verulanus. Much of his wealth would have come from donations to Artemis and the other deities. Some commentators opine that the apostles patronised these particular facilities: others opt for the precursor to the Scholastikia Baths on the main street.

3.5. The Bath as an important institution

In the Roman period there were many baths in Ephesus, both public and private. Considering Map 4A these have been found: (i) beyond the Theatre, (ii) in the Theatre-Gymnasium, (iii) either side of Hadrian's Temple (Centre) and (iv) more were near and beyond the Forum/State Agora (off right).

Baths in the Roman Empire were not just for getting clean: they were important places for physical exercise, socialising, discussing politics, doing business and dining. Bath-houses were associated with social status and Hellenism but, because Jews were supposed to spend as little time as possible there, Jews remained outside the normal social relations fostered by this institution. In fact Jews were expected to immediately immerse in a *mikvah* pool to regain ritual purity because the baths were regarded as contaminating. If an Ephesus synagogue is found, a *mikvah* will probably be found nearby. All bath-houses were impure to Jews because:

> *"Perhaps others had urinated in the water (or worse), impure members of the public may use the facility, public nudity was unseemly and statues of idols and paintings of human figures were the usual decorations in bath-houses. The Mishnah of c.200 CE (m Avoda Zara 3:4) provides another insight.*

Discussions and religious contemplation were forbidden in the bath-house (mMegillah 3:2 and Berikoth 24:4): presumably because Jews were not to loiter in the nude there, perhaps because of temptation and because it was an unseemly place for thoughts about God. Observant Jews would have scrupulously avoided deliberate contamination". (Campbell and Campbell, *Synagoga's Heritage*, 12.9).

**Plate 3.1. Harbour Baths. By Mayer Loigi , 1810.
Public domain.**

It is known that Christians of the 1st century utilised bath-houses because of an amusing incident in the life of St John while he lived in Ephesus. When he arrived and found the heretic Cerinthus was already at the baths he said to his companions: *"Let us get out of here, for fear the place falls in, now that Cerinthus, the enemy of truth, is inside"* (Irenaeus, *Against Heresies* III.3.4).[44] Some commentators assumed that Cerinthus was using the precursor to the large Scholastikia Baths, some say the Harbour Baths, but there is debate about when each of them was completed. There is, in fact, a great deal of confusion about who built which Ephesian baths, and where, and what to name each one. Much attention is paid to Scholastikia's baths, as, although she was a Christian, a brothel may have been included. Her baths could cater for 1,000 patrons and included a library and were not free, but exclusive.

Figure 1 Plate 3.2. Scholastikia Baths, underground level and pipes.43ground level and pipes.43

Plate 3.3. Statue of Scholastikia at her baths.[45]

3.6. Conclusions

Ephesus was a large and extensive city in the Pauline Period and more so later and into the Byzantine (Christian) Period. It was constantly being extended, renovated and rebuilt, especially after earthquake damage. As was usual, material from earlier buildings were scavenged for reuse in later constructions. Not all of the buildings and monuments known to have been in Ancient Ephesus have yet been found by archaeologists but excavation is a work in progress and, as this once magnificent city has long been unoccupied, it is an archaeologist's and a tourist's paradise.

Chapter 4
The Arrival of Christianity

4.1. St Paul in Ephesus

It is almost certain that there was there were some Christians in Ephesus before St Paul arrived in the Spring of 52 A.D. and some believe that the Apostle John was already ministering there and, therefore, was the founder of the Ephesian Church: but there is no evidence that John and Paul were there at the same time.[46] Christianity grew quickly and probably included more than one house-church.

Ephesus was visited a number of times by St Paul during his second, third and his mysterious fourth missionary journeys. He arrived in Ephesus by sea in c.52, returned by way of a land route in c.53, after which he made a short visit to and from Corinth by sea, while residing in Ephesus for about three years (Acts 18:26). Snippets of evidence indicate that Paul also returned for his third visit after being released from his first imprisonment (Eusebius, *H.E.* II.22.6).

4.2. Paul's First Visit in c.52 A.D.

On his first visit Paul arrived by ship, accompanied by fellow tent-makers and Christian leaders, Priscilla and her husband, Aquila. Both were experienced house-church leaders and teachers of 'the way' whom Paul had met in Corinth. Although the couple eventually returned to Rome, Aquila and Priscilla settled in Ephesus and gathered-in any Christians they found to form the nucleus of a Pauline house-church (Acts 18:18). Exactly when the Apostle John arrived in Ephesus is uncertain but his grave is believed to be there.

Plate 4.1. Harbour Road. Photo: D. Campbell.

4.3. What St Paul Saw Upon First Arriving in c.52 A.D.

On his first visit, the first sights to greet St Paul and his party would have been: a lighthouse and the busy port, bustling wharves and harbour-side activities, a building for fishermen to pay their taxes, shops, offices, warehouses, a signal tower and worker's houses.[47] They would have seen the Harbour Gateway (propylon), local workers, sailors and visitors from numerous nations wearing an array of costumes and uniforms. Paul would have understood that this was a cosmopolitan city with maritime trade links that would enable the message of Jesus to spread widely once a church could be established. If people were flocking to this key city to become devotees of Artemis they could also come here and learn about Jesus.

A sizeable population worked on the docks and lived around the harbour, as is demonstrated by the fact that the Harbour Baths and Gymnasium Complex later became the largest in Ephesus and over 360m in length, with two *palaestrae* for exercising (shown on Map 4B).

Plate 4.2. Harbour Road and the Grand Theatre.
Photograph: Dennis Jarvis, 2005.[48]

Paul, Priscilla and Aquila would have walked up Harbour Road (which was later called Arcadiana [as shown in Plate 14.2]). It was a wide, straight, paved road of 530 metres between the harbour and the main city. Along the way they would have seen columns, roofed colonnades and shops. As Plates 4.2 and 4.3b show, from afar they would have seen the Grand Theatre and, as then, on their left, they passed the Theatre Gymnasium complex, which was on the corner with Marble Road. As this very large complex had classrooms, baths and exercise facilities for the exclusive use of theatrical performers it indicates that Ephesus had a thriving Thespian culture, although the Grand Theatre was also used for civic meetings. The Theatre Gymnasium can be seen on the Map 4A, marked D, and on Map 4B. In c.89 A.D. this gymnasium was joined to the Harbour Gymnasium by a *palaestra* (exercise yard) 500x300 meters in size.

(A) The Grand Theatre, Ephesus

The Grand Theatre has survived from Antiquity relatively well. This was the theatre in which the events of Acts Chapter 19:21ff were played out. The acoustics of Greco-Roman theatres are excellent so there was no need for amplification with a megaphone when Alexander or the *grammateus* (mayor, but usually translated 'town clerk') addressed the multitude (Acts 19:33-40).

The theatre was cut into the hillside and was commenced before the turn of the eras. It was being increased in diameter under the Emperor Claudius (41-54 A.D.) and it was this version of the theatre that St Paul would have known. It would be extended to its final size and seating capacity (of perhaps over 24,000) during the Emperor Trajan's period (98-117 A.D.).

The remains visible (to the right of Plate 4.3a) on Harbour Road included the gymnasium and school for performers in the theatre. This area also included the Forum (shown on Map 4A) and may also have included a synagogue. Paul preached in a synagogue (Acts 18:19) but no synagogue has yet been found. Some artefacts bearing Jewish symbols (such as the menorah) and stone vessels (preferred by Jews)[49] have been found in this area[50] and a menorah carved into one of the steps of the Celsus Library attests to a Jewish presence in Ephesus in the 2nd century A.D.

Plate 4.3a. Grand Theatre looking down Harbour Road.

Beside the Grand Theatre there was a Fountain House, which pre-dates Paul's arrival and which is decorated with Ionic columns which are visible in Plate 4.3b. Such houses supplied fresh water and were used to keep food cool.

St Paul's party would not have turned left in front of the Grand Theatre but, if they had, they would soon have passed the Forum, the Stadium and then on to the Cayser River that is outside the city limits.

The Stadium was near the Koressos Gate in the city wall on one edge of town where the poor may have lived (although that area has not been properly excavated).

In front of the Grand Theatre the party obviously turned right into Marble Road. Pedestrians had to avoid the Marble Road by climbing up steps and walking on an elevated stoa or colonnade (*scole*) recently built by Nero (54-68) (Plate 4.4). They then went down steps at the other end. Marble Road was an important street and part of the Sacred Processional Way that circled its way through the city from the eastern entry-gate of the city through the city to the northern gate and on to the Temple of Artemis. (The route is shown on Map 5a).

Plate 4.3b. Fountain House and Grand Theatre above it.[51]

St Paul's party may have stayed on the main roadway and have walked along the elevated, covered scole beside the Marble Road (because this road was used only by vehicles and animals).

Plate 4.4. Marble Road with a *scole* to the right.
Public domain.[52]

If, however, they had entered the Agora/Markets through one of its back gates they would have exited it at a grand gateway, the Gate of Mazaeus and Mithridates (Plates 4.5 and 4.6). They would then have been standing in the Triodos Square where three streets met. If they looked up the Embolos (the lower part of The Curetes Street) Marble Road would be on their left. Paul's party may, however, have stopped to look at the Commercial or Lower Agora on their right as this would have been important to them. It was a place for buying food of all kinds (spices, nuts, grain, fruit, fish and meat) and goods of all kinds, including leather good: a kind of giant supermarket. This would be the market-place that Priscilla and Aquila would, perhaps, soon know very well.

The perimeter of the Agora had roofed colonnades with about 100 booths for shops and there were columns all around the perimeter because columns trumpeted the wealth of a city (even when they had no practical purpose). The Lower Agora was humming with customers and produce arriving and leaving and sellers hawking their wares in loud voices. The wealthy elite would have sent their slaves to purchase goods in this agora as it was rough, busy, crowded, noisy and perhaps smelly, with food-scraps and manure to be cleaned up.

Plate 4.5. Lower Agora and Mazaeus - Mithridates Gate. [53]

The great and famous Library of Ephesus (just visible in Plate 4.5) would eventually be built beside the Lower Agora but when Paul arrived that site contained the Heroon of Androcles (noted below in 4.6) and an octagonal mausoleum for Arisone IV, the half-sister whom Queen Cleopatra dragged away from the Artemision to be murdered, at some time between 40 and 20 B.C. [54]

Plate 4.6. Gate of Mazaeus and Mithridates, Ephesus.
Photograph: D. Campbell.

(B) Gate of Mazaeus and Mithridates, Ephesus.

The inscription on the attic of the splendid triple-arched Gate of Mazaeus and Mithridates is in Greek and Latin and says that it had been built at the turn of the eras by two former slaves as a tribute to the Emperor Augustus his wife Livia, his daughter, Julia, and her deceased husband, Agrippa, in thanks for their freedom. It indicated to passers-by that, in Ephesus, even freed slaves could become sufficiently wealthy to give the city a lavish gift, such as this civic ornament.

The Gate was splendid for the times and functioned as a triumphal arch over the Sacred Way until that Way was rerouted because the Celsus Library had to be built nearby.[55] So that the Library and its scrolls would not be flooded the Mazaeus and Mithridates Gateway, which is at the bottom of the Embolos, had to be lifted for the addition of subterranean drainage. This Gateway provided entry to the Commercial Agora and in the years to come St Paul would often have walked through these archways to purchase food or clothing. It is highly probable that he and Priscilla and Aquila sold some of their leather products here but it is most unlikely that they worked as tanners here because that industry is extremely smelly. One of the purposes for which public latrines were erected was to collect human urine for use in the tanning industry.[56] Food, such as meats and fish, would not have been willingly purchased in such an environment.

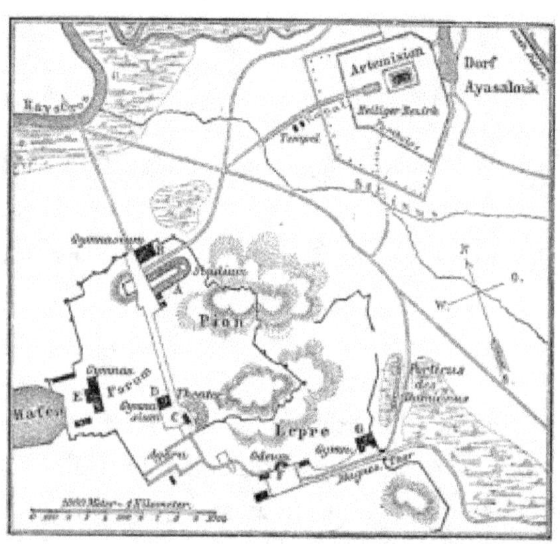

Map 4.A. An Austrian map of the earliest discoveries. Hellenistic city walls and inner Byzantine walls are shown. Stadium (A), Theatre (C), Odeion/Odeum (F) and four gymnasia (B, D, E, G) are marked. The western Forum and Agora/Market are noted. The State Agora at F is not named. Harbour Road from the Harbour/Hafer to the Theatre is missing.

Map 4.B. Lower City

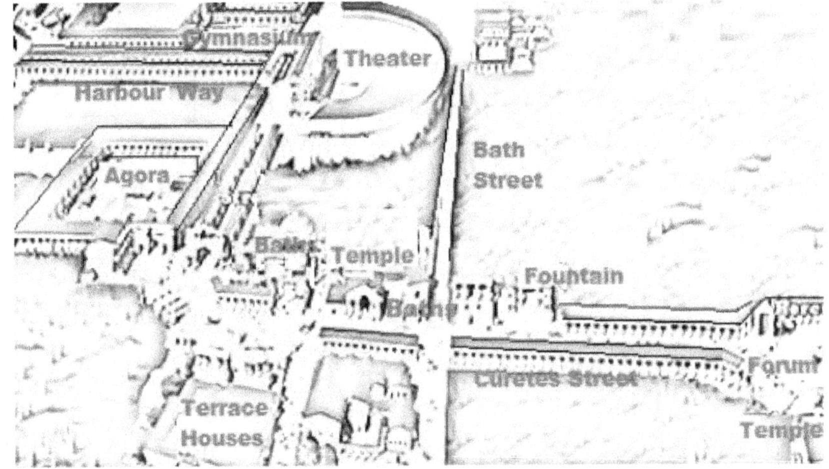

Map 4B shows Paul's first walk from the Harbour (far top left) to the Theater/ Theatre, then into the Agora or right, along the *scole* **of Marble Road to its junction with The Curetes Street, called Triodos Square (where the Celsus Library would be built).**[57]

Although Harbour Road from the wharf to the Grand Theatre is missing from Map 4.A it is marked in blue on Map 5a and the route taken by Paul's party can be traced on Map 4B.

St Paul's party was now in the heart of down-town Ephesus and one cannot say where they went next but finding accommodation would have been the next challenge. There was a residential area on their right: two sections of terraced houses with mosaic-floors, most of them for the very wealthy set, each built around an atrium (central courtyard) and some with bathrooms and internal latrines (Plate 6.1). These houses are described and illustrated in Chapter 6. These wealthy families may have had house-guests, but never lodgers. For that Paul's party would go off the main street to the side streets or further away from the centre of the city to where ordinary townsfolk lived.

4.4. Donations That Assisted the Supply of Water

In the hot climate of Asia Minor and with an ever-growing population water was always an issue of concern to all levels of society. Self-promotion and social welfare went hand in hand. We know that there were numerous wealthy people in Ancient Ephesus, sufficiently wealthy to pay for large structures to be erected for the welfare of the city.

Gaius Sextilius Pollio built the two-tiered Marnas Aqueduct to bring extra water from the Marnas River to a fountain in the city, between A.D. 4 and 14.[58] Many decades later, a Water Palace was built by the proconsul Laecanius Bassus on the South side of the State Agora to store water for the city. It was built in honour of Gaius Ofillius Proculus. Laecanius Bassus then converted Pollio's funerary monument into a fountain in Pollio's honour. As well as these, fountains such as the one called Trajan's Fountain (Plate 1.1) were donated to provide free water to the citizens.

4.5. Other Major Donations

Other donations to the city were decorations in praise of a person and/or his family or of a deity. The Memmius' family's monument on the Curetes Street (Plate 5.6) is an example of the former. As noted, in c.4 B.C. the ex-slaves, Mazaeus and Mithridates, built the triple-arched gate to the Commercial Agora as a gesture of thanks to the Emperor who had freed them (Plate 4.6). Generations of the family of Tiberius Julius Celsus built the Celsus Library from 114 A.D., primarily as his mausoleum. Theirs was the kind of family who lived in the palatial homes on the great stone terraces facing the lower Curetes Street, which will be considered in Chapter 6.

4.6. The *Heroon* of Androclus and Mausoleum of Arisone IV

The, now lost, monument to Androclus the mythical founder of the city, was built in the 2nd century B.C. on the lower end of the Curetes Street in front of the terraced houses on the lower slope of Mt Koressos.

This street was part of the Processional Way and in an important part of the city. The *heroon* was of two storeys with a gabled roof and it did not contain a burial chamber.[59] Beside it stood the pyramid-topped octagonal mausoleum of Cleopatra's half-sister, Arisone IV, who was murdered while Mark Anthony and Cleopatra were in Ephesus, even though Arisone was seeking refuge in the Temple of Artemis (Josephus, *Ant.* 15.4.1).

4.7. Conclusions

Ephesus was a city to be proud of. It was not a planned city but was constantly being added to and embellished, especially by wealthy citizens. As in today's cities, wealth was most evident in the centre of the city, where many fine buildings and monuments were displayed. Many of them, however, post-date the Pauline period.

The grid layout that the Romans favoured was not used overall and, in any case, the landforms were not suited to it. The land rose steeply on either side of the main street, the Curetes Street, as Plate 5.7 indicates. This means that, during rains, water flowed downhill towards the Commercial Agora (Markets) and its entry, the Mazaeus and Mithridates Gate of Plate 4.6. The Celsus Library would be saved from flooding, at great expense, but the Commercial Agora, being relatively flat, would have suffered after each heavy rainfall.

Chapter 5
St Paul's Subsequent Visits to Ephesus

5.1. Paul's Second Visit in c.53 A.D.

At the end of his first visit to Ephesus St Paul promised that he would return (Acts 18:20). He did so in c.53 A.D. and stayed there to evangelise and teach, first in the synagogue for three months and then in a rented lecture hall. This means that his first converts were Jews and, given their monotheism and knowledge of the Hebrew Scriptures, they formed the nucleus of the Pauline church. Paul remained in Ephesus for about three years.

On his second visit, St Paul and his companions entered the city by road from Phrygia, passing through the eastern gate. This had been built by Lysimachos with only one entryway of 3.5m in width which held up traffic and was dangerous for vehicles, pedestrians and animals so that it would be replaced by the Magnesian Gate of three entryways during Vespasian's reign (69-79 A.D.).[60]

5.2. What St Paul first saw on his second visit in 53 A.D.

St Paul's second visit was very different from his first. In a sense he was coming 'home': home to his friends Priscilla and Aquila and many people whom he knew, and who welcomed him so that he had no need to search for accommodation. He immediately picked up his teaching role and again began in the synagogue (Acts 19:8). He then launched out in a new evangelistic thrust with the workers who had come with him and the backing of an established group of trusted believers.

This time, as St Paul was arriving from the hinterland by road, no doubt he was looking forward to a visit to the bathhouse to get rid of the dusts of Asia and a refreshing drink and a meal, home-cooked in Priscilla's kitchen. Hospitality was considered a Christian virtue, which, as leaders of house-churches wherever they lived, Priscilla and Aquila exemplified. Paul had probably survived on dry bread and dehydrated fish during his long treks across Asia Minor.

As St Paul neared the city he would have seen the afore-mentioned two-storey aqueduct, built between 4 and 14 A.D. by Gaius Sextilius Pollio to bring vital water into the city from the Marnas (Devent) River. It supplied water to a large fountain near the State Agora from which residents could collect it. St Paul knew that he had arrived when he reached the city walls that had been built in the 3rd century B.C. by Lysimachos who founded the city. The walls defined the city limits but, unlike inland cities, port-cities like Ephesus were difficult to defend because an attack could come from the sea, or simultaneously from both land and sea. The power of Rome had pacified this part of Asia and the border with the hostile Parthians was far away to the East and, while the Roman Empire lasted, the 'Pax Romana' (Roman Peace) ensured security and safe travel. Afterwards, hostile Arab raiders arrived.

As St Paul came to the eastern gate of the city, the Processional Way stretched up the hill to the Artemesian but there is no record of St Paul ever going there: it was foreign territory and he had no need to visit it. He forged straight ahead and he knew the way. In this area Paul saw one of the gymnasia and before he reached the Curetes Street he would pass the State Agora, one of the main features of Ancient Ephesus.

5.3. The Large State Agora with its basilica (Map 1B)

Of the two agorae in Ancient Ephesus, the one for commerce (buying and selling) has been noted but this one, the State Agora, was for business (trade discussions, business dealings and money changing).

This was called the 'Upper Agora' because it of its higher altitude but it was also 'upper class'.

The rectangular State Agora dated from Hellenistic times but was rebuilt during the reign of Augustus (43 B.C.-14 A.D.): well before St Paul's visits. It was a complex of interesting elements connected with the government of the city and its secondary cult: that of Hestia Boulaia.

The people who gathered in this Agora were an entirely different set from those hard-working folk in the Commercial Agora. These were the leisured class, the religious officials, the civic leaders, the provincial leaders, the property owners and the merchants. Wheeling and dealing and politics were their main interests. Business affairs were very important because Ephesus was a great trading city, which is perhaps why there were so many public and private baths, provided for their long discussions more than for their cleanliness.

The North Stoa within the State Agora was called 'the Basilica'. It had been built in the reign of Augustus (c.11 A.D.) by the previously mentioned wealthy Ephesian benefactor, Gaius Sextilius Pollio, and his wife, Ofillia Bassa, and her son, Gaius Ofillius Proculus. Carved heads of the Emperor Augustus and his wife, the Empress Livia, have been excavated there.

Plate 5.1. The Odeion is at rear,
with the Basilica of the State Agora in the foreground.[61]

As in Plate 5.1, the Basilica was elevated up four steps and its foundation platform has survived, along with two rows of columns that are mere stumps. These columns divided the space into a central nave with aisles on either side. The aisles were not as tall as the nave (much like the roof-configuration of early churches). This building was very large (165m long by 73m wide) and may have functioned as a law court.

Today the State Agora itself is mainly a collection of marble ruins laid out in neat rows. It had *stoas* on all sides. One was the Basilica and the one on the East was virtually a covered veranda, supported by columns to provided shelter and shade. The politically important and/or the wealthy people of town, mainly aristocratic men and merchants, thronged about the State Agora when they weren't at the baths discussing their business affairs there, as was the Roman custom for men. There is even a record of Queen Cleopatra being carried about the State Agora in a litter.[62]

On one end of the State Agora the Emperor Augustus had built his temple. The Agora had previously featured another temple, right near the centre. This was probably an Egyptian style building provided by Egyptian merchants for the honour of the Egyptian god, Isis, but when it fell down Augustus refused to permit a rebuild. Egyptian merchants had combined their business in the Agora with their religious observances and they could easily be distinguished among the crowds by their distinctive dress and headwear. (Later, in the Antonine Period [that is, after 138 A.D.] Egyptian immigrants would also build a temple to Serapis beside the Commercial or Lower Agora).

5.4. The Municipal Palace (Prytaneion) of Ephesus

Although other elements were added over time, the Prytaneion probably dated back to the foundation of Ephesus on this site. It would have been protected if at all possible because it contained the sacred flame, which burned at the cult room of Hestia, goddess of the hearth, who was second in importance to Artemis.

At its height, the Prytaneion was a complex of courtyards, pools, gardens, government offices, accommodation and reception and banqueting halls. The main elements of the Prytaneion were: the assembly hall for city leaders to meet in; the Temple of Hestia Boulaia; the eternal flame; the courtyard and the dwellings of the guardians of the flame around the courtyard. All babies were brought here, to Hestia Boulaia's sacred place, to be carried around her altar for a blessing.

Like the Vestal Virgins of Rome the priestesses and priests of Hestia Boulaia, goddess of the hearth, were highly regarded virgins from the aristocratic families and their names were inscribed on the columns. Civic receptions, banquets, religious ceremonies and political business were conducted here. In Ephesus, the cults were integrated into the fabric of government, political life and social life.

Plate 5.2. Remains of the sacred Prytaneion.
Photograph: D. Campbell.

The illustration in Plate 5.2 shows all that is left of this once important and substantial building in the government section of Ancient Ephesus. It is hard to imagine that this scene of destruction was once the centre of political power in a provincial capital and the second most important site in Ephesus, after the Temple of Artemis. It was situated beside the site of the Odeion, which would soon be constructed. Once Christianity became dominant, the cults lapsed and these buildings fell into disuse. The date of the loss of the sacred flame, which burned at the cult room of Hestia Boulaia, is unrecorded but its loss signalled the triumph of Christianity. Much of the material of the Prytaneion was removed in the 4th century to be used elsewhere, such as in the Scholastikia Baths, and columns and some statues were reused on the

Street of the Curetes, where their names can still be read on some of the columns. Much of the Prytaneion is, however, just scattered around on the ground.

Archaeologists have unearthed three carefully buried marble statues of Artemis in the Prytaneion. One statue was small and two were very large. Of the latter, one dates from the late-1st-century A.D. and the other from the early-2nd-century A.D. The statues were probably buried for safe keeping when the cult was being suppressed in the Early Byzantine Period. All are depictions of Artemis as a beautiful woman with multiple breasts or perhaps they are bees' eggs or bulls' testicles (symbols of fertility). This type, as in Plate 2.1, was called 'the Artemis of the Ephesians'.

5.5. The double temple beside the Prytaneion

The Emperor Augusts built two small con-joined temples beside the Pytaneion during his visit in 29 B.C. to honour his adoptive father, Julius Caesar, and the Good Goddess or the Goddess of Rome (Bona Dea/Dea Roma). She was a goddess of chastity, fertility and the protection of the state and the Roman people. There was also an altar there for the worship of Emperor Augustus and Artemis.

5.6. Was there an earlier version of the Odeion?

While ever Ephesus paid its taxes to Rome and maintained law and order it was left to govern itself, although it was not an independent city-state. The Odeion of Ancient Ephesus was one of the buildings used in the process of government: a meeting place for the town council or *Boule*. Before the Odeion was built there had to have been some place for them to meet and it was probably in this sector of town near the other municipal buildings.

It would appear that the usual government of the city state continued past the 2nd century A.D. as the present Odeion was erected by the wealthy Ephesian couple, Publius Vedius Antoninus and Flavia Papiana, who also built baths in the reign of Antoninus Pius, just after 150 A.D. Statues of family members of the imperial dynasty decorated the Odeion and the marble front row seats (identifiable in Plate 5.3) were reserved for councillors. These rows were wider than those in the upper gallery and they feature lions' feet on the ends, which can be seen in this photograph.

Plate 5.3. Odeion or Bouleuterion.
Photograph: D. Campbell.

The Odeion was next to the Prytaneion and the State Agora was opposite them both. The Odeion was semi-circular and built like a small version of the Grand Theatre, but these days it is not as well preserved as the theatre is. Although it could have been used for small theatrical performances, poetry recitations and/or musical performances the Odeion was primarily a meeting place for the town council. Citizens could have observed proceedings from the galleries. It could seat 1,400 people and was probably roofed. Access for the front section was via gates to the left and right of the semi-circular orchestra and for the upper gallery access was through two vaulted staircases. As Plate 5.1 shows, the Odeion was opposite the Basilica of the State Agora but a two-storied *skene* prevented the audience of the Odeion from seeing into the Agora and kept the sound of the councillor's deliberations confined.

5.7. The Baths South of the State Agora

To the South of the State Agora was a large private bath-house; sometimes called the Upper Baths. It was probably built by the sophist Flavius Domianus in c.200 A.D. so it would not have been seen by St Paul. [The term Varius Baths has become useless through repeated misuse, which makes identification of reports in various sources difficult].

5.8. Baths East of the State Agora

Map 4B shows this substantial building near the eastern entry to Ephesus, which came to be known as the Magnesian Gates when it was widened, and rebuilt with a tower. These baths were large, splendid and dedicated to Emperor Antoninus Pius (131-161 A.D.) who was a friend of the owner, so they were not standing during the 'Pauline Period'. There was a gymnasium and classrooms and an altar so that patrons and students could burn incense to the emperor at any time.

**Plate 5.4. Remains of baths East of the State Agora.
Public domain.**

5.9. The Sacred Way

The Sacred Way was a processional route from the Artemision, down through the main part of the city and back to the Temple (shown on Map 5a). Priests who were acrobats and dancers would participate in the frequent ceremonies and processions of Artemis.

The Sacred Way was a processional route from the Artemision, down through the main part of the city and back to the Temple (shown on Map 5a). Priests who were acrobats and dancers would participate in the frequent ceremonies and processions of Artemis.

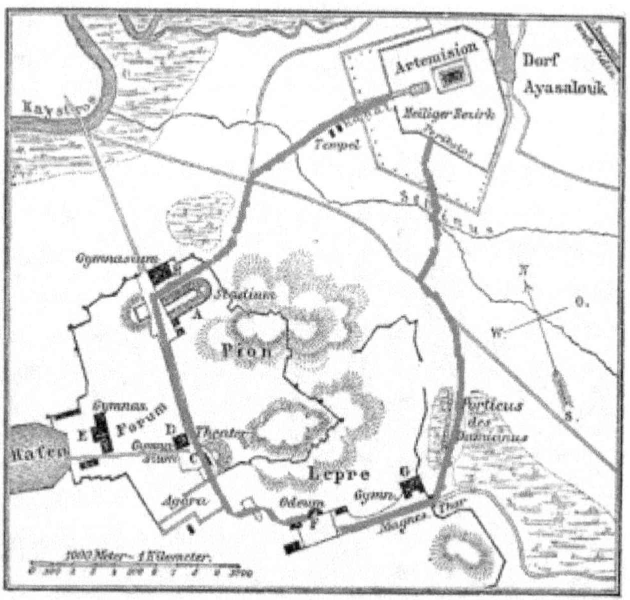

Map 5A. An Austrian map in German (Map 5a) with Harbour Road in blue and the Sacred Way in red but Akurgal and others say that its route went out through the Koressos Gate beyond the gymnasium before turning East.

The Sacred Way began at the Temple, went down to the Magnesian Gate (or its predecessor) at the eastern boundary of the city, wound its way past the Eastern Baths and the State Agora and down the Curetes Street. From Triodos Square it followed Marble Road to the Grand Theatre and beyond, perhaps to the Koressos Gate in the city wall near the river and then returned to the Artemision. This sacred route was a little different in the 1st century, before the Celsus Library was built.

In pre-Christian times it was used for processions in celebration of Artemis each Spring and when games and festivals were held; such as an annual festival of Demeter/Ceres when the cereal crops were to be planted. The eastern section, which is marked *Porticus des Daimianus* on Map 5a, was a covered, colonnaded walkway built in the 3rd century by the sophist Diamianus. In later (Byzantine) times, various saints were buried along this section of the Sacred Way.[63] There had previously been various altars along the Sacred Way where processions would stop for sacrifices of wine and incense and perhaps blood sacrifices.

Plate 5.5. The Sacred Way beside the State Agora.
Photograph: D. Campbell.

5.10. Coming to the Start of the Curetes Street

As they walked on the Sacred Way St Paul and his companions, Gaius, Aristarchus and the others, passed the State Agora and would have seen two prominent hills to the North: Mount Pion and Mount Ayasoluk. The summits of both were fortified by walls, although only the latter boasted a castle, which overlooked the Temple of Artemis. It would later become an important Christian site as the burial place of St John the Apostle over which a great church was built (Plate 15.5b).[64]

Just past the State Agora a temple to Domitian would later be built on an elevated platform, with Domitian Square laid out to enhance it. (It is marked Temple on the right of Map 4B).[65] When Domitian was murdered, his memory was officially erased so the temple was rededicated to his father, Vespasian, so that the city would not lose one of its honours as a 'temple warden' or *neokoros*.

5.11. The Memmius Monument

The Memmius Monument was at the head of the Curetes Street. It commemorated descendants of the Roman Consul Lucius Sulla and dates from the time of Emperor Augustus (34 B.C. - 14 A.D.). Originally, in the 1st century B.C., it was square in shape, on a high, stepped plinth, topped by a square pyramid. It had arches on all four facades, which probably held the statues of the family members, some of which have survived (Plate 5.6); along with a much-photographed bas-relief of Winged Victory extending a wreath.

The Memmius Monument later became a fountain but what can be seen today are the mere fragments of a once tall monument. It was erected in this prominent position on the Curetes Street, near the civic buildings. Along with the surviving statues and reliefs the ancient inscription has survived. It can be translated: *"Gaius Memmius, the saviour, the son of Casius, grandson of Cornelius Sulla."*

Plate 5.6. Monument of the Family of Memmius.
Photograph: D. Campbell.

5.12. The Embolos (Lower Curetes Street)

As St Paul walked downhill to the Embolos (lower Curetes Street) he may have been seen by people who recognised him and he would see the now-familiar grand entrance gate to the Commercial Agora depicted in Plate 4.6, where his friend, Aquila, may have been at work. If so Paul, himself, would soon join him as Paul adopted a principle of working to maintain himself and his friends (Acts 20:34).

In Ancient Ephesus, the Embolos was a main street, adorned with many of the city's notable monuments and buildings. The name 'Curetes' comes from the names and the carved images of the *curetes* that adorn columns along the street (as in the centre front of Plate 5.7). The *curetes* were very important people in the city, including in the time of St. Paul (the mid-1st-century A.D.). As noted, they were priests and priestesses who dealt with civic, political and religious matters.

          DESLEE CAMPBELL

The virgin priestesses were responsible for the sacred, perpetual fire that burned in the Municipality Palace, where they also lived: therefore their names and statues were still firmly in the Prytaneion in the Pauline period.

Plate 5.7. The Curetes Street. Photo: D. Campbell.

The Curetes Street was 1 km long with a sewerage system beneath the paving stones. Today it is lined with columns, and pedestals with statues of *curetes*, other important people and divinities. Originally, behind the columns on the West side there were shops on the ground floors, with living areas above them (as in Plate 6.2). In the 1st century, as today, the street ran downhill from the Heracles Gate to the Mazaeus-Mithridates Gate (Plate 4.6). The great Celsus Library (visible at the bottom of the street in Plate 5.7, and which faces up the street, was only built in the 2nd century although the gateway and the markets (the Commercial Agora) on its left would have been familiar to St Paul. Three streets (Curetes Street, Marble Road and a minor street) met in Triodos Square at the Mazaeus-Mithridates Gate of Plate 4.6.

Some of the imperial monuments on The Curetes Street (such as Hadrian's Temple and Trajan's Fountain, shown on Map 4b as 'Temple' and 'Fountain') were not yet built, but there were other buildings, monuments, fountains and tombs along the Curetes Street, which have not been fully identified by archaeologists. The shops in Plate 6.2, and some of the terraced houses in Plate 6.1, were completed and the overall effect is much as St Paul found it during the three years that he lived here. As some of the illustrations show, the footprint of the city was restricted by steeply rising hills all around. A grid layout was impossible but this was a Greek city, not a Roman one, and military-style grids were a Roman fixation.

Both The Curetes Street and Marble Road, were part of the Sacred Way. Marble Road was paved with expensive marble under the Emperor Claudius (41-54 A.D.). It then intersected at right angles with the Harbour Road close to the Grand Theatre. These three roads were the main commercial streets of Ephesus but Harbour Road was not part of the Sacred Way which led straight past the Grand Theatre to the Stadium and towards the Koressos Gate in the city wall and back up to the Temple of Artemis, as Map 5a indicates.

As St Paul found out to his discomfort (Acts 19:21ff) the Artemis Cult was very prominent, but the Imperial Cult would begin to make inroads, especially later in the century when the Emperor Domitian (81-96 A.D.) built his temple and an ornamented square in front of it. Other cults (e.g., of Serapis) were introduced and became rivals of Christianity, and it is proposed that the cults of Artemis and Isis merged in some way.[66] The religious scene was never static.

     DESLEE CAMPBELL

5.13. The Communal Latrines

In Ephesus, as today, latrines and bathing facilities were situated near each other and many had a gymnasium attached, and perhaps a brothel. Facilities such as public fountains, baths, and latrines for men would have been patronised by Paul and his fellow-Christians such as Gaius and Aristarchus (Acts 21:29). Poor people may have used cess-pits, but the homes of the walthy had a water supply and could have a private privy.

Plate 5.8. Latrines in Ancient Ephesus.

Photograph: Carole Raddato.[67]

Public latrines were all similar: a marble bench with a hole cut in it. Public latrines were set in walled, unroofed courtyards and had no privacy barricades, nor cubicles. They had running water beneath the marble seats and in the open channels at the patrons' feet (visible on the right of Plate 5.8). Patrons used sponges and took water from this channel, but their feet did not get wet. They were protected from the sun by overhanging coverings.

The people of Ephesus were averse to toileting smells and sounds: an orchestra played in Scholastikia's latrine and all public latrines were built unroofed and open to the air.[68] The wealthy might have private latrines in their homes but they were quite different: small and dark and perhaps under stairs.[69] It was fortunate that Ephesus had a number of public baths, as tanners would have needed to bathe frequently. St Paul, having been trained as a Pharisee, would probably still associate cleanliness with godliness but, if he was a tanner as well as a leather-worker, he would have been ritually unclean and smelly most of the time.

5.14. The Synagogue and the lecture hall of Tyrannus

St Paul obviously found the synagogue and the lecture hall of Tyrannus but modern archaeologists have not... yet. This demonstrates that there is much further archaeological work to be done. No synagogue has been identified, although some evidence of Jewish habitation has been found.

5.15 Paul Made a Brief Visit to Corinth

As noted elsewhere, during this period in Ephesus St Paul made a brief voyage straight across the Aegean Sea to visit the church in Corinth, a congregation which caused him great concern. Paul wrote I Corinthians from Ephesus and told the Corinthians that he faced a much opposition in Ephesus but also had a wide open door for ministry (I Cor 16:7ff).

5.16. St Paul's Last Visit in c.56 A.D.

Although Luke said that the Ephesians 'saw his face no more' (Acts 20:38) this indicates that he wrote these words before 56 A.D. and they were true as far as Luke knew at the time. Luke could not have known that Paul would be released from his imprisonment in Rome and have many more adventures in diverse places. Luke did not record them in Acts; or perhaps the record was an appendix that has been lost.

St Paul's final visit was probably a sea voyage as he had been on Crete with Titus (Tit. 1:5) and, as Crete is an island, he could only leave by ship. Paul then visited a number of places, including Ephesus.

From here Paul and Trophimus visited Miletus but, when Trophimus became very ill, he had to be left behind (II Tim. 4:20). It is quite possible that Paul and Trophimus had walked from Ephesus to Miletus as it was about eighty km. Paul then sailed from Miletus to Macedonia and Greece and he was taken into custody somewhere along the way.

5.17. Conclusions

It is difficult to grasp the size and monumentality of Ephesus by looking at the scattered remnants of single buildings. This city was seriously important and many individuals were seriously wealthy. This is illustrated by the sculptures and intricate carving on the stonework of the 2nd century Celsus Library, the third largest library of the Ancient World, which was also a mausoleum.

The task of excavating the city is ongoing and virtually everything has undergone a degree of restoration but one can still walk down the streets that the saints trod and see the same vistas that they saw: the mountains, valleys, rivers and caves; and some of the same buildings.

Chapter 6
Domestic Dwellings in Ancient Ephesus

There is still much to learn about domestic arrangements and homes of Ancient Ephesus as so much of the city has yet to be excavated and because the ancients left few records about trivial matters, which were women's affairs.

6.1. Houses of the Wealthy on the Embolos

As is usual, the standard of dwellings in Ephesus depended upon money. Those of the poor have not been excavated while the few houses of seven very wealthy families are in a fairly good state of preservation, and are now roofed over for their protection (Plate 6.1a) and some are open to the public (Plate 6.1b).

Three strong stone terraces were built into the lower slope of Bülbüldağ (Mt Koressos). On these, relatively well-preserved houses of the wealthy were built. They provide great insight into the lives of at least this small segment of Ephesian society. To begin with, in the 1st century A.D. houses A and B were built on the pre-built terraces. Others were built virtually on top of the first few but leaning back into the hillside. External staircases up both sides gave access to the rear houses and each house had internal stairs to their bedrooms and guest-rooms on the second floor.

**Plate 6.1a. Small shops and houses
on the lower Curetes Street.**[70]

The houses were built in insula style squashed together in a semi-irregular fashion with rooms clustered around courtyards and one room leading into another without hallways. Some rooms were tiny and/or irregular in shape. Some houses may have been more than two storeys high. All were supplied with water and there was a drainage channel under the alleys on either side. Some houses had bathrooms, latrines, fountains, central heating through pipes in the walls and hot water. House A, which had at least twelve rooms around a courtyard on the ground floor had a heated bathroom with a bathtub and also a kitchen and a triclinium for dining.[71] There was little evidence of kitchens in some houses so meals may have been catered for and brought in (like ancient uber-eats) or perhaps everyone ate out, such as in the private bath-houses.[72] The slaves and domestic servants of each family lived in the smaller rooms, some of which are little bigger than cells. Presumably a house with a large number of cell-like rooms indicated a large and/or extended family in each household, or many slaves and servants.[73]

Archaeologists find it hard to determine which rooms belong to which house as it appears that there were doorways between adjoining homes. The name of one homeowner was Gaius Furius Aptusa who was a priest of Dionysus (the god of wine). Houses were repaired and/or reconfigured after the earthquakes of 31 A.D. and 358 or 368, and continued in use until the 7th century.

Plate 6.1b. Interior showing mosaic floors, painted walls, column bases and stairs.[74]

In its simplest form the house had a central courtyard on the ground floor which, unlike many, was not decorated with mosaics and was relatively small, but some had large halls (basilicas). The courtyard was the sole source of natural light for the surrounding rooms as rooms had no windows. Some rooms or halls were built behind others but were very dark because the only natural light came from the courtyard. Rear rooms were accessed through the better-lit rooms. Privacy was not a feature of Ephesian life. The exact configuration of upper floors is unknown.

These homes were meant to be impressive as they were used for entertaining, and for meeting clients and business associates, so they functioned as an office, perhaps for multiple members of an extended family.

6.2. Artefacts in the Terraced Houses

By far the most frequently found artefacts in these seven houses were large and small images of different deities, including beautifully sculpted images of Artemis as a huntress. Carved bas reliefs once decorated some of the walls. Floor-mosaics and portable artefacts commemorated Alexander the Great, Androclus, Socrates and other heroes, and deities. One house held medical equipment and a box of cosmetic paraphernalia. Jewellery was commonly found, including in inexpensive materials for children. Numerous lamps of glass, pottery and metal were found, many decorated with images of deities. These were essential for lighting the inner rooms.

6.3. Interior decorations:

(A) In some houses the walls were covered with marble. In others the walls were of bricks, plastered over, or painted. The plaster was then painted in a style found also in Pompeii, with the walls divided into rectangles by borders, within which flowers, birds, animals and figures of deities were painted. The large 'whole of wall' scenes that were so popular in Pompeii are, however, lacking. Upstairs rooms had similarly painted walls.

(B) Many floor areas were covered with expensive mosaics; mainly featuring mythological figurative scenes and images of heroic figures, such as Socrates, the Spartan philosopher, Cheilon, and the poetess, Sappho. Mosaics featuring geometric patterns changed over time from Greek styles to a more severe geometric style under Roman influences.

(C) Fountains and marble columns decorated the internal courtyards of the more lavish homes. Peristyle courtyards were surrounded by columns.

(D) Some houses had niches to display large statues.

6.4. Insula behind the shops on the Embolos

The housing photographed in Plate 6.1a is of two distinct types: the homes of the wealthy are covered (roofed over). The row of twelve small shops and the houses behind them are much more degraded and are not covered. The ground-floor plan in Plate 6.2 applies to this, exposed section. These shops and houses are visible beside the white roof in Plate 6.1a.

Behind a covered colonnade twelve small shops were built on the lower Curetes Street (called the Embolos). Many of the shops had staircases to access rooms above. An insula of houses squashed together was built on the terraces. One house, with a large peristyle courtyard, was the home of a wealthy person (front right of Plate 6.2, in red). Others were for middle-class people and were smaller and/or had smaller rooms, and perhaps even no courtyard. Some may have been only a few modest rooms. The exact boundaries of each house are hard to decipher and some rooms appear to have had no doorways, or perhaps had a hob that people stepped over. The houses were reconfigured over a period of seven centuries.

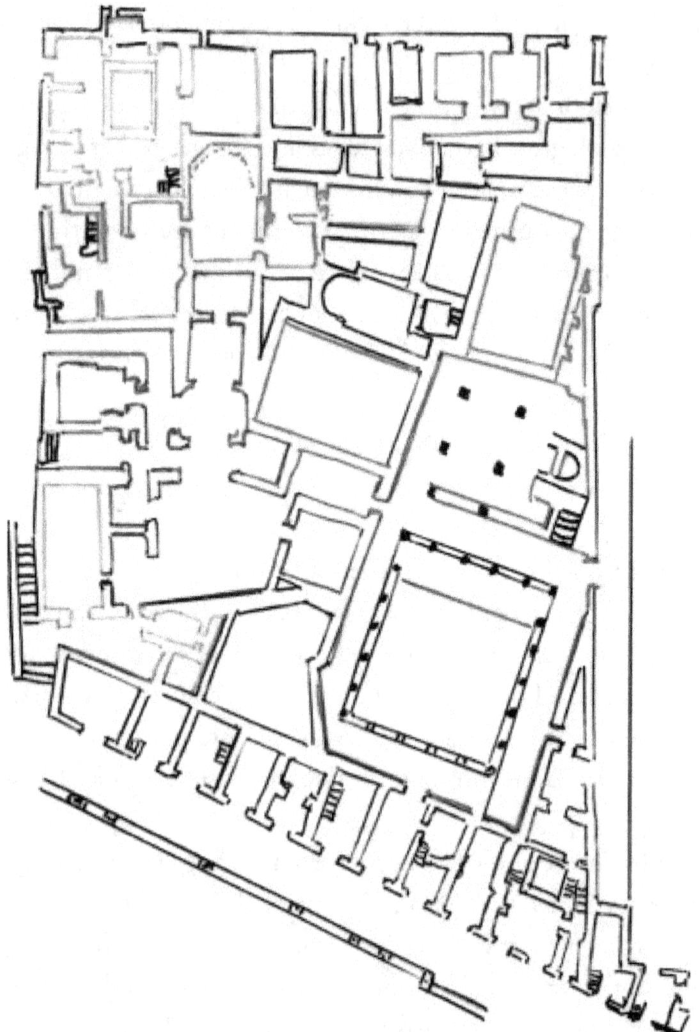

Plate 6.2. Insula behind the row of 12 shops on the Embolos. Shops and Houses to the left of Plate 6.1a.

6.5. A Wealthy Villa with a View

There are various side streets that attract little attention. They include a side street (now called Bath Street) which is narrow but paved and runs off Curetes Street. The Scholastikia Baths (and its predecessor) could be accessed from both of these streets. Bath Street ran uphill to the top of the Grand Theatre where a large villa has been excavated above the Theatre. It is likely that there were other substantial houses up there as the wealthy might have built homes on the cooler heights, to take advantage of the breeze and the commanding views.

6.6. Housing Above Shops

Shop-owners lived above the twelve shops shown in Plate 6.2 and mentioned in 6.5 above and also above the shops on Marble Road, Harbour Road and near the Eastern Gate. To guard their wares day and night, some stall-holders may have slept in their shops in the Commercial Agora (market place).

6.7. Others who lived where they worked

i) Workers who lived near or at their work included the priests and priestesses of the cults, notably those of Artemis and Hestia Boulaia.

ii) Workers who sold vegetables and fruit probably lived on their farms and vineyards in the hinterland valleys. Agriculture would have been a family affair with some members being producers while others sold the produce.

iii) People of the Mediterranean and the Aegean have always obtained the bulk of their protein from the ocean or rivers and those who sold eels, fish or other seafood would have lived near the rivers, lakes or the ocean and brought their catch to market the next day or salted or dried it for subsequent sale.

6.8. Housing areas for ordinary citizens

The oldest houses would have been near the harbour and there were substantial housing areas near the State Agora, near the eastern gateway and near the Koressos Gate. It is probable that poor people lived away from the main, colonnaded streets, perhaps on unpaved roads that may not have survived. Some suburbs that were based upon a grid pattern are known to exist near the city gates but only major buildings have yet been excavated.

6.9. Domestic artefacts

In general, by far the most frequently found domestic artefacts are made of pottery, which is fortunate as this is easily dated by style and scientific analysis. Pottery is also an excellent indicator of wealth as crude local ware contrasts so markedly with expensive fine, decorated and imported ware (which also indicates how widespread the city's trade links were).

6.10. Conclusions

Outer suburbs of the city have not been excavated so homes for the poor have not been revealed but seven insula-style courtyard dwellings for the very wealthy have been found, cleaned and some have been opened to the public. These were commenced in the 1st century B.C and were added to, varied and rebuilt until the 7th century A.D.

They reveal a lavish lifestyle with considerable money spent on interior decoration and great attachment of these families to a variety of deities and heroic figures. These homes survived relatively well because they were covered by a landslide. Separate from these, but close by, was an insula for people of more modest wealth. They are smaller and have not survived nearly as well.

Chapter 7
Priscilla, Aquila and St Paul

7.1. What is known about Prisca (Priscilla) and Aquila?

1. They were a married couple but there is no suggestion that they had children.

2. Aquila was from Pontus on the Black Sea. He and his wife Prisca (whom Luke called by the diminutive form, Priscilla [little Prisca]) settled in Rome (Acts 18:2). Paul called her both Prisca (Rom. 16:3 [see f/note in the NIV]) and Priscilla (I Cor. 16:19 and II Tim 4:19).

3. They worked with their hands as tent-makers/leather-workers, as did Paul.

4. Priscilla's name often precedes Aquila's so she may have had higher status, or have had some independent wealth, or was much better educated, or was a natural leader, or all of these closely associated qualities.

5. They were Jewish and had been expelled from Rome by the Emperor Claudius in 49 A.D., along with other Jews.

6. They were early converts to Christianity in Rome before they met Paul in Corinth.

7. Paul lodged with them and worked with them in Corinth (Acts 18:3).

8. They were hospitable.

9. They ran a house church in Corinth (Acts 18:1-3).

10. They accompanied Paul to Ephesus where they settled (Acts 19:19).

11. Paul was associated with them for two to three years on his second visit to Ephesus.

12. A house-church met in their home in Ephesus and they sent warm greetings to their former church in Corinth (I. Cor. 16: 19).

13. After meeting the Jewish evangelist, Apollos, in the synagogue of Ephesus and hearing his eloquent preaching Priscilla and Aquila knew that his knowledge of Christianity was incomplete and inadequate (Acts 18:26). They took Apollos aside to teach him more about Jesus. Perhaps Priscilla was the main teacher.

14. Apollos and his Jewish converts probably joined Priscilla and Aquila's group.

15. Priscilla and Aquila were in Ephesus while Paul lived there for three years.

16. They returned to Rome and ran a house-church in Rome when Phoebe the scroll-carrier arrived with Paul's major epistle in c.55/56 (Rom. 16:3).

17. II Tim 4:19 indicates that Priscilla and Aquila were back in Ephesus: perhaps to oversee their business interests there.

18. Somewhere they had risked their lives for Paul (II Tim 4:19).

19. Although they moved about, Paul always knew where they were. He called them his 'fellow-workers' and he was very close to them both.

7.2. Paul's first visit

There are a number of noteworthy incidents during St Paul's first, and especially during his second and his final visits to Ephesus. His first visit was during his second missionary journey. It was brief. Paul preached in the synagogue and his message pleased people so much that he was asked to stay longer. He promised to return, God willing (Acts 18:20f).

7.3. Paul's Second Visit to Ephesus

Paul's second visit lasted about three years so this visit was more eventful. In the chronological order provided by Acts they are: 1. He met a group of about twelve disciples of John the Baptist whom he taught the full message of Christ including Christian baptism in water and in the Holy Spirit so that they spoke in tongues and prophesied (Acts 19:1-7).

2. Paul taught in the synagogue for three months (19:8).

3. Then Paul took his disciples and moved to the lecture hall of Tyrannus where he taught for two years (19:9-10).

4. Paul performed extraordinary miracles of healing and exorcism (19:11f).

5. The seven sons of the Jewish priest Sceva were injured trying to copy Paul's exorcisms (19:14).

6. People repented of evil deed, including of magic, and burnt their books of spells (19:18f).

7. Demetrius the silversmith promoted opposition to Paul and caused a riot. Gaius and Aristarchus were dragged to the Grand Theatre and people shouted in unison 'Great is Artemis of the Ephesians' for two hours before two men tried to calm them: Alexander, a Jew, and the grammateus (mayor/town clerk) (19:21-41). Some other high officials, who were Asiarchs, sent Paul a message urging him not to go to the theatre. [The town clerk was like the mayor: a well-known

top official, which is why he was able to quell the riot. Asiarchs were provincial officials as Ephesus was the provincial capital during the height of its prosperity.] Their concern for Paul's welfare indicates that Christianity was reaching the highest levels of power, which was not unusual.[75]

8. Paul decided to leave the city.

7.4. Paul's securely dated imprisonment in Caesarea Maritima

One of the securely datable incidents in the book of Acts took place when Paul was in Jerusalem with a number of delegates from the Greek, Macedonian and Asian churches to deliver their gifts to the Jerusalem church. Paul was arrested and taken under guard to Caesarea. Both governors in turn, Felix and his replacement, Festus (who arrived in 59 A.D.), wished to appease the Jewish Sanhedrin and so kept Paul in prison for two years. Because Paul thought that he would be handed over to the Jews, he, being a Roman citizen, appealed to Caesar (Acts 25:10).[76] He wanted to visit Rome (19:21) and the Lord had told him that he would go there (23:11). This was a fortunate decision because Festus died in 61 A.D. and, while his replacement, Albinus, was still coming from Egypt, the High Priest took the opportunity to kill James the Lord's brother, head of the church in Jerusalem.[77] Had Paul remained in Judea, he may have also been killed then, rather than in 67, or early in 68 A.D., under Nero.[78]

7.5. Paul and his fourth missionary journey

It is generally agreed that Paul was imprisoned twice after appealing to be tried by Caesar[79] but there is more hesitation in claiming that he travelled to Spain. Kenneth Berding has argued that St Paul did travel to Spain, as well as to Crete, Ephesus, Miletus, Troas, Macedonian cities, Corinth and probably Nicopolis before being arrested and returned to Rome where the Emperor Nero had him beheaded.[80] From indications in the later epistles, especially Paul's 'pastoral' epistles, Paul was in Macedonia (I Tim. 1:3), in Crete where he left Titus (Titus 1:5), in Nicopolis (Tit. 3:12), in Macedonia (II Tim.4:13), in Corinth (II Tim. 4:20), in Miletus (II Tim. 4:20), in Troas (II Tim. 1:3) and also in Ephesus (because it is between Troas and Miletus, which may have entailed an overland trip, or a sea-voyage). Paul reported being opposed by Alexander the coppersmith who was still in Ephesus at the end of Paul's life (II Tim. 4:14). Paul was deserted by Demas, Phygelius and Hermogenes (II Tim. 1:15) and received assistance from Onesiphorus (II Tim. 1:18).[81] Some time after sailing North from Miletus, Paul was rearrested and taken to Rome.

7.6. Paul's Final Visit to Ephesus and its aftermath

This last visit was also eventful, with the opposition encountered on Paul's previous visit being reinforced. After he was released from house-arrest in Rome the following occurred:

1. Paul went with Timothy to Ephesus (I Tim. 1:3).

2. In Ephesus, Paul was opposed by Alexander the coppersmith (II Tim 4:14).

3. Phygelus, Hermogenes, Demas and others deserted him (II Tim 1:15; 4:10).

4. Paul may have been arrested in Ephesus but had help from Onesiphorus (II Tim. 1:18).

5. Paul and Trophimus travelled the c.80 kms to Miletus (II Tim 4:20).

6. Paul left Trophimus ill in Miletus and sailed to Troas where he left his cloak, books and parchments with Carpas and then left (II Tim. 4:13).

7. Paul was imprisoned again. He wanted Titus to leave Crete and join him in Rome (Tit. 3:12).

8. Paul requested that Timothy find Mark and bring him to wherever Paul was (II Tim 4.11).

> *"Whether Paul ever fulfilled his intention to visit Spain remains uncertain, although the author of I Clement believed that he did. This epistle was written just three decades after Paul's death and was perhaps written by Paul's co-worker, Clement, who is noted in Philippians 4:3.[82] If Peter was martyred in mid-66 CE Paul may have been away in Spain at the time."* (Campbell and Campbell, *Synagoga's Heritage*, 17.23).

Paul's second imprisonment in Rome was in winter and he sent for his cloak, which he had left with Carpus in Troas (II Tim. 4:13). Unlike his first house-arrest, this time he was in chains (II Tim. 1:8 and 2:9) and endured multiple hearings (II Tim. 3:16). This imprisonment seems more draconian than his first, and more serious. Being a Roman citizen, Paul was probably beheaded, and that under Nero in c.67 A.D.[83]

7.7. Conclusions

The biblical records hint at considerable opposition to the Christian message, much of it aimed at St Paul. Because a silversmith and a coppersmith were implicated in much of this trouble in Ephesus it likely all revolved around the success of Paul's preaching and the subsequent decline in trade connected to the Artemision. This trouble may have been the reason why Priscilla and Aquila returned to Rome for a time, or perhaps they had always intended to return after Emperor Claudius, who had expelled the Jews, had died. Unlike Paul, their ministry seems to have been rather private: within the home-group and in personal one-on-one teaching sessions and providing hospitality for itinerant preachers, including Paul. It is possible, however, that Priscilla and Aquila had business interests that required travel and therefore Aquila was not sufficiently settled to be overseer (bishop) of a church, but one gets the impression that Priscilla was the better teacher or the stronger personality. Women bishops would not have been appropriate in a Pauline church but these two would have been old by the time Timothy became the bishop of Ephesus.

Chapter 8

St Paul's Main Co-workers:
Luke, Timothy, Titus, Silas and John-Mark

8.1. Luke

Luke was St Paul's faithful companion who was with Paul and Aristarchus when Paul was arrested in Jerusalem and then requested to be sent to Caesar (Acts 27:2). Luke remained with Paul during his first imprisonment when some others were deserting him. Luke took care of Paul's health, his physical needs and provided emotional support as best he could but he may not have been present at the very end because the record of Acts terminates before Paul's martyrdom. This leaves so many unanswered questions about how, when and under whom St Paul died, although the bare bones of the narrative can be deduced from hints within the later epistles.

In Col. 4:14, Paul called Luke, 'the beloved physician' and there are little hints in Luke's two records (his gospel and the Acts of the Apostles) such as references to illness and bodily matters, that support the conclusion that he was a medical man. Luke is not called 'Luke the historian' as he did not write history in the way that modern historians wish that he had, but then no one did before Eusebius, Metropolitan Bishop of Caesarea, wrote his Church History in the 4th century. Neverthe-less, Luke's educated literary style, careful historical research and theological skills are admired.[84]

Although Luke carefully researched Paul's biography he inserted himself into the narrative of Acts (which indicates his personal involvement in those particular events). Only Luke was with Paul during his second imprisonment in Rome (II Tim. 4:11) although he did not extend the Acts-narrative to cover that period: but perhaps he did but the text was lost.

8.2. Timothy of Lystra

Timothy, the son of a Jewish mother (Eunice) and a gentile father, was a timid young man who was probably converted during Paul's first missionary journey when he preached in Lystra, in Galatia. Because everyone knew that his father was a gentile, Timothy was circumcised at St Paul's behest (Acts 16:3). The local Christians of Lystra and Iconium spoke well of Timothy (v. 2) and Paul greatly appreciated and warmly praised him (I Cor 16:10; II Tim 3:10ff).

Timothy joined the mission on Paul's next visit to Asia Minor and was with Paul in Athens (Acts 17:14ff). He was sent back to Thessalonica (18:5; I Thess. 3:1-5) and rejoined Paul in Corinth (v.6; Acts 18:5f). Timothy was with Paul in Ephesus during Paul's lengthy stay but had been sent on to Philippi in Macedonia with Erastus before the dangerous riot of Acts 19 broke out in Ephesus (Acts 19:22).

Timothy then went to Corinth (I Cor 4:17; 16:10) and back to Macedonia. Timothy was also one of the party who accompanied Paul to Jerusalem to deliver the donations to the 'mother church', along with Sopater, Aristarchus, Secundus, Gaius, Tychicus and Trophimus (Acts 20:4f; I Tim. 1:3). After this Timothy was left in charge of the Ephesian church. Timothy became like a son to Paul (Phil 2:19ff; I Tim. 1:2). St Paul respected Timothy's grounding in the Hebrew Scriptures (Old Testament) and recognised his potential. Jewish youths, like John-Mark and Timothy, who had been raised by devout parent(s) had received an ideal preparation to become church-leaders in the next generation, whereas converts from paganism had first to overcome the hurdle of making enormous changes to their lifestyle, behaviours, thought processes and ideas.

Paul said of Timothy, *"I have no-one else like him, who takes a genuine interest in your welfare"* and *"like a son he has served with me in the work of the gospel"* (Phil. 2: 20ff). Paul gave Timothy weighty responsibilities in various place: he was sent with Epaphroditus to Philippi (Phil. 2:19, 25); with Erastus to Macedonia (as noted) and on to Corinth (I Cor. 4:17); he was sent to Corinth again (I Cor. 16:10) and was left in Ephesus to oversee the church (I Tim. 1:1-3).[85] Like a number of Paul's friends and relatives Timothy was imprisoned somewhere (perhaps in Ephesus) but was released (Heb. 13:23) which may have given him the status of a 'confessor' (people who afterwards functioned like priests in absolving sins, especially of those who had lapsed during times of persecution). At the end of Paul's life he sent Tychicus to relieve Timothy in Ephesus so that Timothy could bring Mark with him, collect his cloak and documents from Carpas, in Troas, and join Paul (perhaps in Nicopolis) for the winter as the great apostle was feeling isolated, alone and cold (II Tim. 3:11ff).

The apocryphal *Acts of Timothy* indicates that Timothy was martyred in Ephesus for opposing celebrations of the cult of Dionysus, the god of gender fluidity and wine[86] so perhaps he was buried there.

8.3. Titus

St Paul described Titus, a gentile, as 'a true son in their common faith' but much less is known about Titus than about Timothy, although both became overseers (bishops) of important churches: Titus in Crete (Tit. 1:5) and Timothy in Ephesus. In his ministry journeys Titus travelled widely, including to Dalmatia (II Tim. 4:10) and he was given important responsibilities for that 'problem child' the Corinthian church, which Timothy, who was probably younger and certainly more timid, had been unable to sort out. Titus was reliable and mature.

Titus first appears in Paul's story in Gal. 2:1 when he joined Paul's party on the way to Jerusalem,[87] either for a meeting with 'the pillars' or for the later 'Council of Jerusalem' (c.48 A.D.) (described in Acts 15:1-21) but he was clearly already a believer of some importance by that time. In II Cor. 8, Titus is mentioned a number of times for his enthusiastic promotion of the collection of funds for the needy Jerusalem church (e.g., verses 6 and 16f).

Because Paul had rebuked the Corinthian Church for disunity (I Cor. 1:12) and immorality (5:1) he was apparently hesitant about revisiting it so he sent Titus as his emissary to prepare the way and to restore order (I Cor. 1:15-18, 23; 2:12f). Eventually Titus found Paul in Troas and he brought good news from Corinth: the church had repented (II Cor. 7:5-16) which meant that both Titus and Paul were joyful and Titus would return to them with a relieved heart (7:17), accompanied by an un-named brother.

In II Cor. 8:23, Paul describes Titus as a 'partner and fellow-worker among you' (the Corinthians). He did not often travel with St Paul as he was trusted to do mission on his own, as St Paul directed. At the end of his life Paul sent for both Titus and Timothy to join him in Nicopolis for the winter (Tit. 3:12).

8.4. John-Mark

John-Mark, the son of Mary of Jerusalem, was a relative of the disciple Joseph Barnabas, a wealthy land-owner and Levite from Cyprus (Col. 4:10; Acts 12:25; 13:5). John-Mark may have entered the Christian story in the Garden of Gethsemane as many suppose that he was the youth who fled naked when Jesus was arrested (Mk. 14.51). At this very early time his mother was a follower of Jesus and their home became a place of ardent prayer when St Peter was first imprisoned (Acts 12:5-18). These events make the young Mark one of the first people to have been raised in a Christian environment.

The family was sufficiently wealthy to have a large home suitable for a house-church. It also had a courtyard, and they owned a slave woman named Rhoda. The White Russian Church of Alexander Nevsky, off Muristan Road in walled Jerusalem, is believed to mark the location of this house-church.[88] John-Mark had both a Jewish and a Latin name and, like Jewish boys, would have been taught to read the Hebrew of the Bible. He probably read and wrote Greek and he almost certainly spoke the Aramaic of the city streets.

Barnabas requested that John-Mark accompany Paul and himself on Paul's first missionary journey, which was to his home island, Cyprus. All went well until they reached Perga in Asia when John-Mark left them and went home (Acts 13:13). This annoyed Paul so much that he later refused to take Mark on his second journey and Barnabas was replaced as Paul's travelling companion by Silas (Acts 15:37f). Barnabas and Mark then went to Cyprus together (Acts 15:39).

John-Mark matured over the years and his relationship with Paul was repaired. Later he became a great help and companion to Paul, although he was of a younger generation. It is uncertain when Mark's mother became a Christian but Mark may well have grown up knowing Jesus, himself, and all of the inner-circle, not only St Peter.

John-Mark had received an excellent education and had grown up under Peter's teachings and apparently kept in close contact with Peter, who spoke of Mark as *"my son"* (I Pet. 5:13). Mark's real life's work began in Rome towards the end of St Peter's life when he became Peter's scribe and/or translator and later attempted to record everything that he had heard from Peter (Eusebius, *E.H.*, II.15). Towards the end, or after Peter was martyred, Mark wrote down everything that Peter had told him of Jesus' story, which became *the Gospel According to St Mark*.[89] Mark then became important to St Paul. Although Mark was no longer in Rome and Timothy was in Ephesus, Paul instructed Bishop Timothy: *"Get Mark and bring him with you, because he is helpful to me in my ministry*" (II Tim. 4:11) so John-Mark must have been in Ephesus, or nearby.

The historian-bishop, Eusebius (*E.H.*, II. 16) places Mark in Alexandria, founding the church there. Mark later travelled in North Africa and back to his 'ancestral home', Cyprus, as an evangelist. Local tradition places him in Cyrenaica, North Africa, in about 66 A.D. and in nearby Alexandria for his martyrdom in 68 A.D.[90]

8.5. Silas/Silvanus of Jerusalem

Silas, like St Paul, was a Roman citizen. He was an early believer because he was already a leader among the brethren and a recognised prophet by c.48 A.D. the approximate date of the 'Council of Jerusalem' which ruled on the issue of whether believers had to first convert to Judaism (Acts 15:22, 32). Silas was sent with Judas-Barsabbas from Jerusalem as a messenger to the gentile converts in Syrian Antioch both to deliver a letter from the 'mother church' and to give them a verbal report (v.27). Silas and Judas-Barsabbas were able to encourage the believers before returning to Jerusalem (v.32ff) (Acts 14:22-36). Although Silas was not called an apostle he was clearly educated, a good speaker and a mature believer.

Paul chose Silas to travel with him on his second missionary journey into Syria and Cilicia (v.40f) and then to Macedonia where Paul and Silas were both flogged and imprisoned in Philippi. In prison they prayed and sang hymns together (16:25) before being miraculously freed but, because they were Roman citizens who were legally exempt from flogging, the magistrates had to apologise to them (v.38). They proceeded to Thessalonica where the unbelieving Jews stirred up trouble. They hastened to Beroea where the reception was warmer, until some arrived from Thessalonica to make such trouble that Paul was promptly accompanied to Athens, leaving Silas and Timothy in Beroea. When Paul had preached in Athens, including to the city leaders of the Areopagus, he went to Corinth where Silas and Timothy rejoined him (18:5).

Silas is not mentioned in the list of Paul's companions in Ephesus in Acts 20:4 although Timothy is there and presumably also Luke. Silas took only a peripheral part in Paul's story so that his personality is not really revealed. He slips from the story and when Paul was sent from Jerusalem to Rome, to be tried by the emperor, only Luke and Aristarchus accompany him (Acts 27:2). Silas probably returned home to Jerusalem and became close to St Peter. He and John-Mark may have travelled with St Peter to Rome where Peter referred to Silas (in I Peter 5:12) as a faithful brother. Even though John-Mark was with them, it was Silas who was Peter's scribe in writing Peter's first epistle to the Christians of Asia Minor (I Pet. 1:1) and he may have expressed much, or some of it, in his own words.

8.6. Conclusions

Like Jesus, Paul appears to have a small inner circle of disciples and a larger outer circle. The members of the outer circle did not always travel with Paul but moved into and out of his current work, or scattered on various mission trips. As the younger men, notably Timothy and John-Mark, matured they became more necessary to the Pauline mission and personally closer to the apostle.

Of the men discussed in this chapter Luke travelled extensively with Paul and remained with him during some or all of his imprisonments. As Paul faced his coming end he wrote to both Timothy and Titus, separately, asking them to leave the work he had assigned to them and come to him. Perhaps they reached him before his martyrdom under Nero who *"was an execrable and pernicious tyrant"* who *"crucified Peter and slew Paul"*.[91]

Chapter 9

Paul's Staff Members Who Knew Ephesus

9.1. Tychicus, Trophimius, Onesiphorus, Gaius, Aristarchus, Erastus, Onesimus and Epaphroditus

Each one of the men listed here either stayed beside Paul as his personal staff or travelled widely at Paul's command and evangelised or taught the believers according to the local needs and their own skills. They either accompanied Paul on his visit(s) to Ephesus, had been there or knew its church leaders. They are discussed individually below.

They are: Tychicus and Trophimus and Onesiphorus who were Ephesians; Gaius and Aristarchus who were caught up in a riot in the Grand Theatre in Ephesus, Erastus who visited and left with Timothy; Onesimus of nearby Colossae and Epaphroditus, a Macedonian who met the leaders of the Ephesian church in Miletus.

9.2. How Onesimus fits into the story

Onesimus was a runaway slave, who was owned by a Christian, Philemon. Onesimus met St Paul during Paul's imprisonment, probably in Rome. Onesimus became a Christian and was devoted to St Paul who wanted to keep him but it was decided that Onesimus must return to Colossae in Asia to his owner, Philemon. Tychicus would escort him there and deliver a letter from Paul to Philemon. This became the canonical *Epistle to Philemon*, in which the slave-owner is urged to restore Onesimus; and even and even to manumit him.

When St Ignatius of Antioch wrote to the Ephesian church in either 106 or 110 A.D. their bishop's name was Onesimus.[92] If the runaway slave had been a teenager at the time it may well have been the same person, a matter that has excited scholarly controversy. Onesimus means 'useful' and it was a common name for slaves, which suggests that, in any case, the bishop had once been a slave.[93]

9.3. Tychicus of Ephesus

Tychicus, was a Christian convert of Ephesus who was a 'dear brother' to St Paul and a faithful minister (Eph 6:21) who became his reliable and helpful assistant (Eph. 6:21). Tychicus travelled as one of St Paul's party through Greece and Asia (Acts 20:4ff) and, as a representative of his congregation, Tychicus accompanied Paul to Jerusalem with the relief-money Paul had been accumulating (Acts 320:4; I Cor. 16:1-4). Tychicus also accompanied the runaway Onesimus on their journey to Colosse and Tychicus also carried letters to Asia from St Paul.

Tychicus and Onesimus transported three known letters: one to the slave-owner, Philemon, one to Ephesus (Eph. 6:21f), another to Colosse (Col. 4:7ff); as well as the now-lost letter to Laodicea. Although the letter to Philemon was short, even it was not just a few pages of paper. Each letter was a cumbersome scroll, made of vellum or parchment (the skins of calves or sheep) moreover each would have been wrapped in its own leather pouch for protection. The scroll of Colossians would have been over one metre in length and the scroll of Ephesians would have been at least a metre and a half in length. No one knows how long the lost epistle to the Laodiceans was, nor how large or how heavy its scroll would have been.

Based on Wilder's analysis of two Jewish examples from Josephus and five non-Christian authors' accounts of *diakonoi* (couriers, herald or messengers) in the Roman world a letter-carrier also gave verbal reports and explained the written message.[94] Paul's letters were written in *scriptio continua* (without punctuation marks or word-breaks) so that Paul would have had to coach Tychicus in the correct way to read each of the letters so that he could correctly read each scroll out loud to the relevant recipients.[95]

Another task of a Christian letter-courier was to encourage the believers and share information about what Paul and his team had been achieving, which Tychicus clearly did. Paul called Tychicus a *diakonos* (translated deacon, minister, servant, herald or official messenger).[96]

The biblical texts concerning Tychicus elaborate on the task of the letter-carrier (Eph. 6:21 and Col. 4:7-8, Philemon 10, 12).

"Tychicus will tell you all the news about me .... that he may encourage your hearts" (Col. 4:7a and 8b).

"Tychicus, the dear brother and faithful servant in the Lord, will tell you everything, so that you also may know how I am and what I am doing. I am sending him to you for this very purpose, that you may know how we are, and that he may encourage you" (Eph. 6:21-22).

St Paul also requested that letters be shared between congregations (Col. 4:16). The last letter Paul wrote was to Timothy and it was probably delivered by Tychicus whom Paul sent back to his hometown, presumably to take over administering the church. This would free Timothy up to leave and hasten to Paul's side (II Tim. 4:12).[97]

9.4. Trophimus of Ephesus

At the end of St Paul's third missionary journey Trophimus was with him in Jerusalem (Acts 20:4). Being a gentile, Trophimus was the innocent cause of an uproar around the Temple in Jerusalem (21:29) in which the crowd beat Paul and the Romans arrested him, took him to Caesarea and kept him incarcerated for two years.

Epistles written after the events narrated in Acts had occurred indicate that Trophimus was with Paul in Ephesus and that Paul left him ill in Miletus. He was so ill that he could not travel when Paul sailed for Macedonia. As Miletus was about eighty miles from Ephesus, Trophimus was close to the assistance of his friends and relatives and he did recover. This illness did not occur on St Paul's third missionary journey as it is not mentioned in Acts. Indeed, Trophimus was with St Paul and his group when they arrived in Jerusalem so it must have happened after St Paul was released from his first Roman imprisonment.

9.5. Onesiphorus of Ephesus

Presumably Onesiphous was from Ephesus. Certainly he resided there with his household during the Pauline Period.[98] Paul associated him with Priscilla and Aquila in II Tim. 4:19, so he and his family were probably members of the house-church they hosted. His role in helping Paul in Ephesus is rather mysterious and he seems to have been a man of some status in Ephesus. He rendered much service to Paul and was not ashamed of Paul's chains during Paul's second imprisonment when Onesiphorus looked for and found Paul in a prison (II Tim. 1:18).

9.6. Gaius from Macedonia

Gaius may have been an early believer. He was one of St Paul's closer friends and assistants and was linked with Aristarchus in the New Testament record. They were together in Ephesus when the riot that was prompted by Demetrius the silversmith broke out (Acts 19:20). He may have been the same Gaius mentioned in Acts 20 as one of those travelling in Paul's party from Macedonia to Greece and back to Asia but there were possibly four Christians with the name Gaius during the Pauline period so it is impossible to allocate other references to this Gaius with any certainty, but he was certainly with Paul in Ephesus for some years.[99]

9.7. Aristarchus of Thessalonica

Aristarchus, a Macedonian from Thessalonica and a Jewish believer, was with Gaius in Ephesus when the riot broke out against Paul's preaching (Acts 19:20). Aristarchus and Gaius were dragged about by the crowd that gathered in the streets and were then rushed into Great Theatre of Ephesus. They were saved from further punishment by a city official. Aristarchus went on to Jerusalem and was still with Paul and Gaius when they went into Macedonia (Acts 20:4).

Aristarchus was devoted to St Paul as he later accompanied Paul and Luke (when the former was in chains) from Jerusalem to Rome and was a 'fellow prisoner', which may have been a voluntary imprisonment to assist Paul (Acts 27:2; Col 4:10).

9.8. Erastus of Corinth

Erastus does not appear early in the story. He was with Paul in Ephesus and was sent with Timothy from there to Macedonia while Paul stayed on in Ephesus until after the riot promoted by Demetrius the silversmith (Acts 19:22). Erastus probably proceeded into Greece and south to Corinth and he was staying there when the second letter to Timothy was written, shortly before Paul's martyrdom (II Tim. 4:20).

9.9. Epaphroditus of Philippi

Epaphroditus, a gentile, whose name means 'foster child' was a senior member of the church in Philippi, in Macedonia. He was chosen by that church to accompany Paul and six others to deliver the money collected for the Jerusalem church, in c.54 A.D. so he would have been with Paul as he sailed by Ephesus and met its church leaders in Miletus. He carried Paul's letter from Rome to his 'home church', the Philippians (Phil. 2:25-30).[100]

9.10. Epaphras of Colosse

Epaphras of Colosse was a prisoner with Paul in Rome during his first imprisonment (Philemon 23; Col. 4:12). The distance by the road from Colosse to Ephesus is maybe 100 miles and Ephesus would have been the nearest port city, so Epaphras probably sailed to Rome, or an intermediary port, from Ephesus.

9.11. Conclusions

This group of dedicated disciples and assistants in the Pauline mission were participants in Paul's experiences in Ephesus, both good and bad. Some of them hailed from Ephesus, one was a short-term visitor, two lived not far from Ephesus and three of them were from Macedonia (Gaius, Aristachus and Epaphroditus). Two Macedonians, Gaius and Aristachus, lived with Paul in Ephesus where both had a frightening experience, which they survived. The other Macedonian, Epaphroditus, met the leaders of the Ephesian church at Miletus.

Paul had many such supporters, who dedicated their time and loyalty to his mission, and without whom his mission would have had less success but there were some men who were his soul-mates. They were discussed in the previous chapter and it was their companionship which Paul sought at the end of his life.

Chapter 10
Early Christianity in Ephesus

10.1. The First Christians in Ephesus

As noted elsewhere, the Ephesian church may have been founded by St John. There were probably some Christians in Ephesus when Priscilla and Aquila arrived with St Paul to obtain a house and begin a house-church. This couple continued to attend the synagogue, which is where they met the eloquent Alexandrian preacher Apollos, whom they taught. Luke does not tell us either way, but Apollos may have been baptised in water and the Holy Spirit (although Acts 18: 24-28 says this only of the other disciples of John the Baptist, whom Paul met). House-fellowship would have been maintained, even after the number of converts increased under St Paul's ministry in the city because that was the 'gold-standard' in the Jerusalem church and because Priscilla and Aquila were very hospitable. St Paul evangelised in the synagogue and then in the lecture hall of Tyrannus, during two years of his second visit (Acts 19:10). These were evangelising meetings, not worship services nor Eucharists (Holy Communions). Paul certainly promoted Holy Communion (I Cor. 11:17-22), so that must have taken place in the house meetings and in conjunction with the normal hospitality provide by the host and hostess, as was the case in the 'mother church', Jerusalem.[101]

10.2. Competition From the Imperial Cult

Much is made of how Christianity competed with, and clashed with, the cult of Artemis but the cult of emperor worship was a long-term and growing rival as well. This began with the first emperor

Augustus (Octavian) to whom Herod I built a temple in Caesarea. Augustus also approved the building of a temple in Ephesus to honour his adoptive father, Divus Julius Caesar, and, as the list at 10.3 below will show, numerous other emperors followed suite. Various Roman emperors played an important role in embellishing Ephesus (and their own reputations in the process).

10.3. Imperial Constructions

Augustus (43 B.C.-14 A.D.): Temple to Julius Caesar; Basilica; Triumphal Arch.

Claudius (41-54 A.D.): the theatre; the paving of Harbour Road.

Nero (54-68 A.D.): made changes to the Stadium.

Domitian (81-96 A.D.): built his own Temple.

Trajan (96-117 A.D.): built a fountain with a 57m high statue of himself.

Hadrian (117-148 A.D.): a small temple, his Gate/Arch, the Olympeum Temple

Antoninus Pius (138-161): completed work begun by Hadrian

Marcus Aurelius (169): built the Great Antonine Altar

Constantius (317-361): renovation of the Harbour Baths in this reign

Arcadius (395-408): rebuilt Harbour Road

10.4. The Great Antonine Altar now in Vienna

This largely overlooked monument was a large U shaped altar (like that of Pergamon, which is now in Berlin). The Antonine Altar was constructed by Marcus Aurelius for the imperial cult and to trumpet the importance of the Antonine dynasty, which had been deliberately founded by the Emperor Hadrian (who ruled from 117 to 138 A.D.). It was still clearly worthwhile to expend considerable moneys to provide a large altar for the imperial cult almost a century after St Paul's martyrdom.

Four male and one female figures from the Antonine Altar are visible in Plate 10.1. These imperial figures were related as follows. Hadrian (117-138) inherited the imperium from his adoptive father, Trajan.[103] Being childless, although married, Hadrian adopted an honourable senator, Antoninus Pius (138-151), on condition that he would adopt two lads from important families who would then inherit power and rule jointly. They were Marcus Aurelius (151-180) and Lucius Verus (161-169).[104] In this way Hadrian established the rule of 'the five good emperors' (who included his adoptive father, Trajan [98-117] who is not pictured). The four males depicted in Plate 10.1 are: on the left, Marcus Aurelius (as a lad of 17); Antoninus Pius (as a venerable sage); Lucius Verus (as a child) and Hadrian. The female figure hidden behind Hadrian is Antoninus Pius' daughter, Faustina the Younger, who would strengthen the cohesion of the dynasty by being given in marriage to young Marcus Aurelius.

This imperial altar would have caused great affront to the believers but it indicates that conversion at the grass roots was slow, even in Ephesus where so many Christian luminaries laboured. It was the Christianising of those with imperial power, beginning with Constantine the Great, that quickly terminated the imperial cult and ensured that legislation in the whole empire would swing in favour of Christians and the Church.

Plate 10.1. Dynastic successors of Hadrian
on the Antonine Altar.[102]

The most important high-relief sculptures from the Great Antonine
Altar are now in Vienna. From a Christian viewpoint these rulers were
not 'good emperors', but better than some of their predecessors, like
Caligula (37-41 A.D.) and Nero (54-68 A.D.) but the Jews regarded
Hadrian as a cruel and violent emperor.[105]

10.5. Problematic Elements in 1st Century Ephesian Society

i. The Stadium or Circus

From 69 B.C. gladiatorial fighting with men and wild beasts took place in the Stadium in Ephesus, which the Emperor Nero upgraded in the Pauline Period. Horse races were held in the Stadium but perhaps it was too narrow for chariot races. Sports, athletics contests, ceremonies, boxing, fights to the death and protracted festivals of combat and slaughter were held in it. This meant that a whole industry grew up around fighting; including the importation of wild animals from Africa and the training of gladiators.[106] Untrained criminals were also forced to fight each other.

In 1993 Austrian-Turkish excavations unearthed a training ground for gladiators and also a cemetery in which 68 men between the ages of 19 and 30 and who had died of fatal wounds, were buried,[107] although their skeletons show that some wounds did heal. A *'medic'* assisted with this. Ephesus abounds with graffiti that gladiators left behind. Many of the deceased had carved tombstones with inscriptions, some of which were commissioned by their wives. Some gladiators who lost 'fights to the death' had to kneel or lie on the ground and submit to the fatal blow. Most combatants belonged to their owners who preferred their slave to remain alive to fight again, but some gladiators volunteered for the role because it paid well.

Events were well run and the training was rigorous. In the Ephesus Museum there is a sculpted plaque that depicts two gladiators in combat with a referee standing nearby. Different categories of fighters followed different rules and used different weapons. This popular 'spectator sport' was cruel to the combatants and the animals and was phased out by c.400 A.D. under the influence of Christianity.

ii. Nude Mixed Bathing

Nudity was disapproved of in Judaism and even members of one's family were to be modest, but in the 1st century A.D. in Roman society nude bathing was considered normal and Greek males competed while naked in gymnastics and games (such as in the original Olympic Games). Statues of their gods and goddesses often showed them in 'heroic nudity' and even ruling emperors and empresses were depicted naked. The introduction into Jerusalem of Hellenism, which included these ideas, gave great offence to Jews and was an important motivation in the Maccabean Revolt against the Greek-Seleucids (130-135 B.C) and the two wars that the Jews fought against Rome (67-73 A.D. and 130 –134 A.D).

In the Roman Empire, the use of the bath-houses became a very public affair. It was not without its dangers and some emperors tried to curb mixed bathing but others did not. Roman people bathed daily and also dined in the baths, socialised and held discussions at length there. Their servants accompanied them to the private baths to mind their belongings and to massage their naked bodies; but for themselves, the servants used only the cheap public baths.

In Italy, the public baths at Pompeii and Herculaneum had separate bath-houses, apparently for men and women, but at the turn of the eras the Romans began to have mixed bathing so that, in St Paul's day, different cities, even different facilities, would have had different practices.

Given that St Paul stressed female modesty and decorum it is possible that Christians frequented the baths less frequently than they had done before their conversion but Bishop Clement of Alexandra (c.150-c.215) was the first Christian leader to express concern about mixed bathing, although others followed. Some suggested that women should use the baths at night to avoid males. In the 4th century, St Jerome said that virgins should be too modest to see themselves naked and that married women should not go to the baths because pregnant women look disgusting.[108] St Jerome's friend, St Paula of Bethlehem, never took a bath: because of her extreme asceticism, not her physique, even though she was the mother of five children.

iii. The Rites Associated With Cybele

As has been noted earlier, Cybele's cult was prominent in all of Asia and was integrated into the religious landscape of Ephesus. Even pagan Rome was opposed to this cult, the male devotees of which castrated themselves and indulged in wild orgies of self flagellation.

iv. Slavery

Enslavement of non-Romans was widespread through the Roman Empire and slaves could be purchased cheaply after the captives from a newly conquered area flooded the slave-markets. One well-know example of this is that most of the Jewish residents in Rome were freed slaves, originally captured by Pompey in 63 B.C., or by Titus in 67-73 A.D. When slaves were plentiful and cheap, even a slave could own a slave. St Paul did not confront slavery head-on but he was kind towards the runaway slave, Onesimus, offered Philemon recompense if anything had been stolen and he tried to influence Philemon to free Onesimus (Phil. 18, 21).

10.6. Conclusions

Paul was not a social reformer he was a reformer of the soul: one soul at a time. His focus remained on his chief calling and he did not seek-out conflict on other matters. There were many aspects of Ephesian life that converts from paganism took for granted but which were contrary to both Christian and Jewish morality. Except for his concern about women's dress and behaviour, which are trivial compared with slavery and fighting against people and animals for entertainment, Paul did not confront or oppose these elements.[109] He concentrated on bringing change within each person: promoting the inner virtues, which he praised in his circular letter, known as *Ephesians*: truth, kindness, love, humility, gentleness, patience, purity and unity.

Chapter 11

Paul, Ephesus and Jesus' Message to the Church in Ephesus

11.1. Paul Writing to the Corinthians about his time in Asia

In writing to the church in Corinth Paul mentions some of his experiences in Asia (including in Ephesus) but these are so incidental that most scholars have interpreted them as metaphors rather than as real events. They include that he was in deadly peril (II Cor. 1:10), that he was afflicted and utterly, unbearably crushed (II Cor. 1:8), that he fought with wild animals at Ephesus (I Cor. 15:32) and that his life was in danger in Asia (II Cor. 1:9). If any or all of these applied, literally, to Ephesus than St Paul had a very difficult time there.

11.2. Epistle to the Ephesians

Paul's Epistle to the Ephesians is a wonderful little book. It is the whole story of the Eternal God's romantic relationship with his dear ones, neatly tied up in one package and closed with a ribbon and a bow. "*The Epistle to the Ephesians is all about the glory of God*".[110]

Unlike Paul's other epistles, especially the one to the Roman church, it does not single out individual people for either commendation or reproof so perhaps it was a circular letter, general in nature, to be shared between the usual seven suspects (as were the letters in Revelation 1:20 to 3:22). Perhaps, however, that personalising of the message in most Pauline epistles was a rhetorical device to draw in people whom he may never have met, which was not necessary when Paul was writing to a congregation who knew him so well.

Even if this letter was destined to be shared around it would have certainly arrived in the port city first, so that group of recipients, the church in Ephesus, would have been in Paul's mind during its composition as he could not be certain which other congregations would be given it, nor how long that would take.

The universality of the message means that it has had universal meaning down through the centuries, as much now as back then. One note of interest in the text is that there was a previous, brief letter that has been lost (Eph. 3:1-3).[111] Apparently it contained Paul's testimony of his conversion and/or personal commissioning in the Lord's service.

Perhaps, also, insights into his later encounters with the risen Christ, such as the one recorded in Acts 22, which took place in the Jerusalem Temple. This encounter is noted in our book, Justin Campbell and Deslee Campbell, *Synagoga's Heritage: Tabernacle, Temple, Synagogue and Church* (2020) 11.10, as follows:

> *"A few years after the Resurrection, Jesus visited the Temple to meet St Paul although he could have met Paul anywhere, at any time. The encounter demonstrates that Jesus did not spurn the Temple. It is perhaps even more surprising that Paul, who was newly converted to 'The Way', went to the Temple to pray. Jesus went there: to meet with this new convert, to respond to his supplications and to give him orders that would save his life:"*

Paul was told: *"Leave Jerusalem immediately because they will not accept your testimony about me"* (Acts 22:17-21). Perhaps that brief lost-letter to the Ephesians recorded Jesus' assurance to Paul when he had been arrested in Jerusalem that he would be a witness in Rome, also:

"The following night the Lord stood near Paul and said, 'take courage! As you have testified about me in Jerusalem so you must also testify in Rome'" (Acts 23:11).

We have Luke's perspective on these events but it would be even more illuminating to have Paul's own record. The loss of this manuscript means that four of St Paul's epistles are lost: the one to Ephesus; two to Corinth and one to Laodicea.

11.3. Paul and the Pastoral Epistles

Paul's tone in writing the three so-called Pastoral Epistles is quite different from the others and therefore his vocabulary is different, which has led some to contest Pauline authorship. He is an older man, under heavy imprisonment, facing death and his scribe may have had some latitude in composing the text. The personal messages he sends show his close connection to Timothy, Titus and others: they are among his closest, most loyal supporters.

11.4. St John's Letter to the First of the Seven Churches: Ephesus

The letters from 'John the Elder' that are recorded in Revelations 2:1ff, started with Ephesus and followed a circular route from one city to the next in the order in which they are named. The personal message to each congregation was different: short but individualised. Their apostle-bishop, the elderly John, knew his churches well and addressed their strengths and weaknesses. The prophetic word from the Lord to Ephesus was as follows:

"To the angel of the church in Ephesus write: These are the words of him who holds the seven stars in his right hand (i.e., the angels), and walks among the seven golden lamp-stands

(i.e., the seven churches). I know your deeds, your hard work and your perseverance. I know that you cannot tolerate wicked men, that you have tested those who claim to be apostles but are not, and have found them false. You have persevered and have endured hardship for my name, and have not grown weary.

Yet I hold this against you: You have forsaken your first love. Remember the height from which you have fallen! Repent and do the things you did at first. If you do not repent, I will come to you and remove your lamp-stand from its place. But you have this in your favour: You hate the practices of the Nicolaitans,[112] which I also hate. He who has an ear, let him hear what the Spirit says to the churches. To him who overcomes I will give the right to eat from the tree of life, which is in the paradise of God" (Rev. 2:1-7) .

Bishop Irenaeus, in *Against Heresies* III.3, stated in around 185 A.D. that St John the Apostle lived into the reign of Trajan (98-[119]) and, in the 4th century, St Jerome noted that St John had lived to such a great age that he had to be carried into the Christian meetings in which he always exhorted them to ' *love one another*'.[113] This time-line does not require that there be two elderly leaders, both named John.

11.5. Conclusions

Compared with the church on the island of Crete, whom Paul described as rebellious, mere talkers deceivers, liars, vicious brutes, evil beasts, lazy gluttons and false teachers (Tit. 4:12f) the church of Ephesus was a well-taught and well-disciplined congregation. Their main teachers had been: St John, St Paul, St Timothy, St Luke, Priscilla and Aquila and perhaps Philip the deacon and some of his four daughters. St Paul loved this congregation and desired to return to them, but he suffered much in doing so.

Chapter 12

Did Paul's time in Ephesus influence his views on women?

12.1. Paul's deep familiarity with Ephesus

As argued elsewhere in this book, as a Christian leader, St Paul, spent more time in Ephesus than in any other city, including Rome, Corinth, or perhaps Jerusalem. Some scholars allocate three and a half years to just one of his periods of residence. It is not an exaggeration to say that Ephesus was Paul's favourite city and his favourite church. Given that length of time, Paul had an opportunity to take stock of the popular culture. He did not immerse himself in the culture but he would have come to understand it and to see how the Jewish and Christian minorities functioned within it. He would have noted each and every festival, procession, sporting event and celebration in the local annual cycle and to have experienced their mourning rituals in which women with loose hair, mutilated faces and, with naked breasts (which they constantly beat) followed funeral processions to signify that death was the end of virtue and beauty.[114]

12.2. Paul, Christian Women in Rome and the Church in Rome

Paul had never been to Rome when he wrote *The Epistle to the Romans* but he knew quite a lot about its people. He sent greetings to ten women leaders: Prisca, Junia, Mary, Tryphaena, Tryphosa and Persis, who were his co-workers, and also Julia, Olympas, the mother of Rufus who was a mother to Paul also, and Nereus's sister (Rom.16:12-16). Paul had obviously met a few of them previously: Mary, *"who bestowed much labour on us"* (Rom. 16:6) and of course his co-worker, Junia, *"outstanding among the apostles"* (Rom.16:7) who was probably married to Andronicus, both relatives of Paul and whose preaching engagements landed them in prison with him (Col. 4:10).[115]

Two other women leaders were particularly noted by Paul: Euodia and Syntyche, who were probably deaconesses in Philippi, in Macedonia.[116] They were having a disagreement, yet they attracted praise from Paul who called them *"loyal yolk-fellows who have contended at my side in the cause of the gospel"* (Phil. 4:2f). Phoebe, who carried the five metre long scroll of this letter from Corinth to Rome, attracted the highest praise from Paul: even greater praise than other women, for her work and her leadership:

> *"I commend to you our sister Phoebe a servant* (deaconess, messenger or minister) *of the church at Cenchreae. I ask you to receive her in the Lord in a way worthy of the saints and to give her any help she may need from you, for she has been a great help to many people, including me"* (Rom. 16:1).

Paul accepted the leadership that had arisen in Rome. There is no hint in *The Epistle to the Romans* that Paul ordinarily opposed women's leadership, even the apostleship of Junia, so there must have been something very different about Ephesus.

12.3. Strong female participation in pagan cults in Ephesus

As previously noted virginal, high-born women could be priestesses in the Artemision. At least fifteen women even became chief priests in Ephesus and some women became high priestess of Asia.[117] This was a matter of great status. By the time of Paul's visits to Ephesus, women could also hold positions of status in the imperial cults.[118]

Furthermore, women were in complete control of the cult of Bona Dea (the Good Goddess) so that men could not even know her name. The priestesses of Hestia Boulaia lived on-site and helped guard the eternal flame that represented the spirit of the city and this role combined political power with religious status.[119] Some women were among the *curetes* whose names and/or statues now decorate the Curetes Street.

Each year in Fall/Autumn, married women left their families for three days to indulge in the Thesmophoria, a festival of the goddess Demeter/Ceres, to grieve the loss of her daughter Persephone at the time the grain-crops were planted. It seems to have been a kind of all-girls-orgy of fun, stupidity, vulgarity and bawdy behaviour.[120] Wine was consumed and private and secret rituals were enacted.[121]

In the cult of Bacchus/Dionysus women left their families and followed the god into the mountains where they would revel, and dance as maenads, ecstatically. This reinforced the belief that women were volatile and irrational beings who needed close control.[122]

12.4. Paul's advice to Timothy about women in II Tim. 2:9-15

In his later epistles Paul was much more concerned with women - how they behaved and what they wore - than he had been earlier (especially when he wrote to the Roman church which had many prominent women, whom Paul praised).

Because Paul was writing to Timothy while his young protégé was the overseer (*episcopi*) in the church of Ephesus it was the local situation that prompted the topic and was the background to his communication. The believers of Ephesus, both men and women, were 'baby Christians' and many of them brought their cultural baggage from paganism with them. Perhaps more than other cities in Asia Minor, women had a more notable role in the cults and religious practices of Ephesus and the city had a prominent role in Asia, setting an example of women with spiritual power, which the men accepted as normal and natural. Perhaps their secrecy also worried Paul. Both male and female cult-leaders were more powerful, more wealthy and perhaps better educated than elsewhere. This probably led some of the women to be outspoken and to automatically assume a role of power, as naturally befitted their status and wealth.

Because Christianity utilised a written Scripture, the Hebrew Scriptures, a high level of literacy was required, but most Ephesian women were either illiterate or, at best, had only four or five years of schooling. It was Christianity and the need to be able to read and interpret the Scriptures and teaching materials that soon promoted the need for widespread education.

For ordinary married women if their main, regular 'religious' experience had been participating in the Thesmophoria, or the worship of Cybele (which included the outcry of wolves and lions, loud laments, frenzied shouts of war dancers with swords, timbrels, cymbals and drums, merrymaking and orgies)[123] the Christian meeting would have been strange territory.

Although the Temple of Isis, which had stood in the centre of the State Agora, was no longer standing, women were important in the cults of Isis and Artemis in teaching, and in propagating the beliefs and rituals, which included that man was the one deceived, not Artemis. In the Artemis cult it was believed that the goddess was the author of man and, in the myth of Isis, because she deceived Ra and usurped his authority, she obtained greatness and power.[124] Paul's intimate knowledge of the local situation in Ephesus was fuelling his ideas and his vocabulary.

Was St Paul trying to prevent any transfer of pagan behaviour into the congregation when he wrote that women should *"not usurp authority over men"* (I Tim. 2:12, AV/KJV)? Isn't this somewhat superfluous because even men should not 'usurp authority' in the congregation?

Interestingly, Lurie Kimmerle draws attention to Paul's unusual use of the Greek word *authentein*, which mean 'dominating authority', and is different from 'moral authority' (*exousia*).[125] This usage was clearly intentional, yet Paul's words have been used to reduce women's contribution to that of silent observer in some churches, even today, and, secondary to that, to intimidate some inter-denominational ministries into curtailing women's active participation.

It seems that the true meaning of Paul's warning is watered down in some versions of the Bible in English to "*have authority over men*" (RSV; Good News; Amplified) or "*have authority over a man*" (NRSV; NIV). This completely changes the meaning from "*usurp authority*" and "*dominating authority*". No one, however, can be certain if Paul meant this verse to apply to a wife and her husband or to any woman and every man; or all men as a group, because the Greek word for wife and woman is the same and that for husband and man is the same.

The Wycliffe Bible's translation of the 14th century is equally correct "*but I suffer not a woman to teach, nor to have lordship on the husband*", while the Orthodox Jewish Bible says "*I do not allow a wife .... to have dominion, taking authority over **her** man.*" If all of the translators had all chosen to use the worlds 'wife' and 'husband' rather than 'woman' and 'man' how different would the church have been for almost 2,000 years?

12.5. How Christian women should dress

When St Paul required modest and suitable dress, the pagan religions are again in the back of his mind. Wealthy women, who were closely associated with the Artemision, or had come out of that cult into Christianity, wore ostentatious and expensive clothing and much jewellery, as Artemis also did. Yet many Christian women were servants, slaves, ex-slaves and/or illiterate working women who were poorly dressed and probably ashamed of how they looked. Paul wanted to avoid this disparity. He could not give poor women pearls, but he could ask the rich not to flaunt them.

Plate 12.1. Roman woman of the 1st century..[126]

As to the topic of hair styling, the richest Roman women had female slaves whose sole job was to care for the mistresses' hair. In the 1st century many glamorous, complicated and extravagant coiffures were created. Women wore wigs of human hair and gold-dust was sprinkled in the hair of the uber-rich. As in Plate 12.1, their hair was always meticulously groomed.

When the empress had a new style, rich women's *ornatrices* copied it and the style gradually spread around the empire, by which time the empress had a different one. Some extant sculpted busts of Roman empresses demonstrate the trends: some busts had a removable stone wig that could be changed as her hairstyle changed. Poor women, however, could barely manage to keep their hair washed. Paul's desire for unity, harmony and an egalitarian spirit in the church motivated his advice. He did not aim to put rich women down but to elevate humble women and reduce their embarrassment.

12.6. Discussion

Today, Christians read all Pauline epistles with the same mindset but each was nuanced for the particular recipients as each culture was different. Well-known Baptist theologian, Ben Witherington III, said this about Paul's various letters, *"we must always remember whom he (Paul) is addressing"*.[127] The Church in Rome was not a Pauline church. It was strong before he ever went there and its leadership patterns were well established and he accepted that and neither criticised nor interfered. Paul arrived as a prisoner and, as far as is known, he never attended a meeting of the congregation so that his ministry was limited to personal meetings with individuals and small groups who came to visit him. Priscilla, the teacher of Apollos, had previously been a member of the church in Rome and Paul greatly admired her and called her a familiar term, 'little Prisca' (Priscilla).

12.7. Conclusions

Although each city had its female deities, no city was as totally engrossed in and committed to a goddess as Ephesus was to Artemis and because Ephesus was, for some time, a provincial capital and other peoples flocked to the Artemision, its influence was strong and widespread and its priestesses' power rivalled that of the Vestal Virgins in Rome. By comparison with the many mature Christian women of Rome to whom Paul wrote personal messages, gentile women who converted in Ephesus needed much guidance, teaching and behaviour-modification.

Chapter 13
How Did Christianity Change Ephesus?

13.1. Ephesus did not change quickly

Christians had no political power while ever they were being persecuted under the pagan emperors, moreover the old Ephesian beliefs, cults and customs continued for centuries. Consider, for example, the East Gymnasium and its attached Vedius Baths which were built in A.D. 150 on the eastern edge of town by Publius Vedius Antoninus. This was a century after Christianity arrived in Ephesus. This large, complex, bathing facility contained classrooms for boys from six to sixteen, the usual hot, cold and temperate pools, dressing rooms, lavatories and furnaces in the basement to provide steam and hot water. Standing statues identified as the sophist Flavius Damianus, dressed as a priest of the imperial cult, and of his wife, Vedia Phaedrina, were found in the baths so they may have been connected with its construction (as was the case in two other examples of baths). He was a friend of the 2nd century emperor, Antoninus Pius, so these baths were dedicated to Antoninus Pius and to the goddess Artemis. It included a cult-room for pagan religious observances with a central niche, which probably held a statue of the said emperor. As an altar stood in front of the niche, patrons and students could offer incense to the emperor at any time.[128]

In the 2nd century the same prominent Ephesians were also involved in the construction of two other baths, although these lacked facilities for cultic practices. The Private Baths near the Odeion was small, but an inscription indicates that it was constructed by the said sophist Flavius Damianus.[129] At the opposite end of the city, near the Stadium in the North, there was a small, similar building, also associated with Publius Vedius Antoninus, but commentators tend to confuse the three baths.[130]

Public bathing continued into the Christian era as two sets of baths were added to Ephesus in the Byzantine period: in the 4th century Scholastikia upgraded a bathing complex opposite the homes of the wealthy on the Embolos (lower Curetes Street) (Plate 15.1) and the Byzantine Baths probably date from the 6th century.

13.2. The City changed when Christian buildings were built

At first churches would have been small and were overshadowed by the great temples and public buildings and gymnasia but, if these older buildings were damaged by earthquakes they became ruins and eventually disappeared because their marble was reused elsewhere. In the 6th century, under the Emperor Justinian, the great church of St John (in Plate 15.5a and b) was built. It announced the importance of Christianity.

In modern times, attempts at reconstruction the ramshackle Fountain of Trajan have taken place. Some of the ancient stones have been salvaged but Plate 1.1 demonstrates how unsuccessful this has been because of the losses over two millennia. Trajan's oversized foot indicates how large his image originally was.

13.3. Notable Byzantine-Christian sites built from the 4th century onwards:
1. Church of Mary (Plate 15.3).
2. Church of St John (Plates 15.5a; 15.5b).
3. The Scholastikia Baths (Plate 15.1).
4. The Cave or Grotto of St Paul (15.6)

5. Tomb of St Luke.
6. Cave of the Seven Sleepers (15.8)
7. New City Walls.

Other Byzantine Buildings

1. Church dedicated to the Archangel Gabriel.
2. Church dedicated to St Timothy.
3. Church dedicated to St Paul.
4. Church dedicated to St Luke.
5. Church dedicated to St Marcus (which has not been found).
6. St Mary's House (Plate 15.4) (date unknown).

13.4. Christianity Changed the Religious Landscape

Over a few centuries, the temples of the old beliefs and their cults dwindled in importance and observance. Eventually the cult centres, such as the Artemision and the Prytaneion, fell into disuse and then decay so that their fabric was removed and reused, including for the building of numerous new churches and buildings owned by Christians. One notable example of this is that identifiable material was taken from the Prytaneion (including its Temple of Hestia) to be reused by the Christian businesswoman, Scholastikia, in the reconstruction of her private three-storey baths, latrines and brothel (Plates 15.1). Similarly, the columns containing the inscribed names of the *curetes* were reused by the city to decorate Curetes Street.

13.5. Did Christianity Change the Government?

As Christianity increased in Ephesus the bishop became more important to civil society and a substantial bishop's palace was built on the road to the Stadium. Church officials gradually replaced the town council and other officials in administering civic affairs. Eventually the buildings used for government and political purposes fell into disuse and, as noted, their fabric was scavenged and reused elsewhere and some of their sites were reused for churches.

13.6. The Nature of Civil Society Changed

Paul's two canonical epistles to Timothy were written while Timothy was leading the Ephesian church and they would have influenced his teaching and preaching. They contain many admonitions about acceptable behaviour: in general the display of wealth was vulgar and vanity in women was unChristian. These were revolutionary concepts in a city noted for its wealth and the heady pursuit of wealth and in which social class was largely communicated by women's clothing and presentation. In other words, the dress-code was quickly changed and the values-system that had defined Ephesus was gradually overturned.

The violence with which Paul's preaching was opposed indicates that Ephesus was being shaken to the core. Previously new cults had been able to coexist with old ones but Christianity demanded a complete turning away from old ways: a complete conversion.

13.7. Discussion

As Paul wrote in II Cor. 1:8f, he had a very difficult time in Ephesus, which he described as *"fighting with wild beasts"* (I Cor. 15:32). The Christians there also faced strong opposition, but they remained faithful. Gaius and Aristarchus might well have been killed during the riot, perhaps Timothy was imprisoned there (Heb. 13:23) and Paul might even have been imprisoned there, as the apocryphal *Acts of Paul* states.[131] Indeed there is a site there which is called "Paul's

Prison". Ephesus had an arena but it **was** the arena. In the 1st century there was a clash of gods: a contest for many souls.

Although there was some penetration of Gnostic ideas this was not a disorderly 'problem church' like Corinth, nor one, like the Galatians, that was so led astray by strange ideas that St Paul had to rebuke it: but the triumph of Christianity was not solely because of Paul's ministry. Many of the key early Christian personalities contributed to the growth of the Ephesian church. Obviously Mother Mary and St John, Jesus' cousin, would have brought their unique narratives and insights whenever they spoke, although Epiphanius (375 A.D.) expressed doubt that John took the Virgin to Ephesus. The tradition has, however, endured. Christianity did not triumph, however, until imperial policy changed in its favour, beginning with Constantine I (312-337). Persecution of Christians ceased with the edict of Milan in 313 A.D. and Christianity became the official religion of the Empire under Theodosius I (379-395).

13.8. The Contribution of St Ignatius of Antioch: Bishop and Martyr

About one decade after St John had died, St Ignatius, Bishop of Antioch, wrote to the church of Ephesus as he was passing by on his way to be martyred by wild beasts in the arena in Rome. His epistles have survived, and this one confirms the previous picture of the Ephesian believers: their unity, their endurance and their soundness of doctrine.[132]

13.9. Conclusions

From the mid-1st to the late-4th-century, and especially by the 6th century, Ephesus changed radically: its outward appearance, its popular culture, its religious observances, its form of government and its government instrumentalities. It was also changed in mind-set: people no longer flocked to the Artemision but to the grave of St John and the churches. People's behaviours changed: even to how women fixed their hair.

Chapter 14
How did Ephesus Change Christianity?

14.1. Ephesus facilitated the spread of Christianity

A. Christianity spread into Asia Minor, **the great hinterland of the port and along the caravan routes that fed gods and produce into it (Acts 19:26) so that** *"all of the Jews and Greeks who lived in the Province of Asia heard the word of the Lord"* (19:10).

B. Christianity spread into Macedonia, Greece and the Aegean Islands along the shipping lanes that fanned out from the port as Christians travelled north and west by sea.

14.2. Ephesus set an example for other churches to follow.

Because its people were so well taught and shepherded by the great ones Ephesus demonstrated the unity, love and patient endurance in the face of opposition and suffering for which they were commended in Rev. 2:2f and by St Ignatius of Antioch, bishop and martyr, in his *Epistle to the Ephesians.*[133]

14.3. Paul's strictures about Ephesian women have impacted all churches ever since, because the women converts, who had left the Artemis cult, were assertive, and not as docile as most. They were *"assertive, competitive, vocal, and well-versed in their religion"* and actively promoted the myth and also competed to attain important roles.[134] Paul's rule about women being silent were, however, taken to such literal extremes that some later churchmen (e.g., Tertullian) forbad women even to voice their singing.

Catherine Booth, the co-founder of the Salvation Army, wrote a spirited and bible-centred defence of women's ministry in which she demonstrates that women's prophecy, prayer and teaching were permitted in the Early Church and were not the prattling, chatter, arguing and/or babbling that apparently went on in Ephesus, and which St Paul censured.[135] If Catherine Booth wrote this article unaided she was indeed a well read, intelligent and original thinker, although her opinions may have been inspired by a previous prominent woman, Mrs Margaret Fell Fox, co-founder of the Quakers.[136]

14.4. Ephesus was a useful training ground for Paul's assistants.

This congregation was led by an array of luminaries and was so supportive, that, as they participated in the work, men like Gaius and Aristarchus could see how a church should function.

14.5. Ephesus was one church that the youthful Timothy could manage.

When Paul heard of the troubles in Corinth Timothy had been sent there (I Cor. 4:17) but he had been unable to restore order and harmony so that Titus had to be sent to take over (II Cor. 8:16f). Timothy had much better success as overseer (bishop) of the church in Ephesus (I Tim. 1:2-3). Although false doctrines were circulating in Ephesus, Timothy's depth of knowledge (attributed to his mother and grandmother) and his commitment enabled him to oppose these (I Tim. 1:4-11).

14.6. Conclusions

Ephesus crystallised and exemplified many facets of Christian belief and practice. Their meetings were apparently so well run that their praxis did not cause Paul concern. They had been well led for about half a century when they were commended by St John the Elder. They were wise and knowledgeable about the faith and were able to detect and silence false teachers, they were hard working and tenacious.

At the end of the 1st century, when St John the Elder wrote his brief commendation to them in Revelations they had loyally survived a tough period of persecution. They had, however, lost their first love, a condition that did not have to be permanent (Rev. 2:4).

Chapter 15
Remains and Archaeological Discoveries

15.1. Some important Byzantine-Christian sites built or used from the 4th century or afterwards that have been noted are:

1. Church of Mary (Plate 15.3).

2. St Mary's House (Plate 15.4).

3. Church of St John built by the Emperor Justinian (Plates 15.5a; 15.5b).

4. The Scholastikia Baths (Plates 15.1).

5. The renovation of Harbour Road by Arcadius (Plate 15.2)

6. The Cave or Grotto of St Paul (Plate 15.6).

7. The Cave of the Seven Sleepers (Plate 15.8).

8. The Tomb of St Luke.

9. St Paul's Prison.

10. Rebuilt City Walls.

11. The Hercules Gate.

12 Church dedicated to the Archangel Gabriel.

13 Church dedicated to St Timothy.

14 Church dedicated to St Paul.

15. Church dedicated to St Luke.

16. Church dedicated to St Marcus (which has not been found).

15.2. The Scholastikia Baths in Ephesus

Scholastikia was a very wealthy 4th century Christian lady who acquired public baths that dated back to the late 1st century (towards the end of the Apostolic Period). In about 400 A.D. Scholastikia extended and restored this into an up-market private facility for up to 1,000 people.

Originally it was near a public latrine that seated 50 people simultaneously, along with a brothel. This all seems to have been incorporated into the Byzantine period baths. There were other baths in Ephesus, including in the same city block, but Scholastikia's were off the Curetes Street on the corner with Bath Street, in a central position, opposite the homes of the wealthy.

Scholastikia's baths were three storeys in height but, of them, only the ground floor has survived. It had three pools (for cold, warm and hot water) and a room for sweating. There were no extra pools to be reserved for women, as it was a male domain. A library, a relaxing room and a gymnasium were included: quite a home-away-from-home. The brothel apparently occupied the upper floor.

All of this raises many questions about how Christians (and Jews) really functioned on a day-to-day basis in the great cities of the Roman Empire. Meanwhile, as noted, back in Jerusalem, strict rulers about nudity and use of bathhouses had been implemented.[137]

Plate 15.1. Remains of the ground floor of Scholastikia's Baths.

Photograph: Bernard Gagnon. 138

5.3. Harbour Road, later rebuilt by Emperor Arcadius

Harbour Road was restored by the Byzantine-Christian Emperor Arcadius [395-408] so it was renamed Arcadiana, but it would have been very ancient at the time of his intervention. Arcadius did not just repave the Road but entirely remodelled it. The width of this street, 11metres, indicates its importance and the amount of traffic that it catered for: vehicles, animals and pedestrians. The artist's reconstruction in Plate 15.2 indicates how the Arcadiana appeared in the late-4th century.

Plate 15.2. Harbour Road rebuilt as the Arcadiana in the late-4th-century.[139]

15.4. Byzantine-Christian Churches

So far about twenty churches have been unearthed in Ephesus. In the Byzantine Period, the bishops of Ephesus gained power, controlled the town council and used public sites for new churches. Furthermore, the once great temples were deserted, destroyed by the Goths and left to decay, or were rifled for reuse, or the marble stones were ground down for lime, leaving little trace.

15.5. The Church of the Virgin Mary

Churches that have been excavated below their original ground level were all found to have been built over earlier buildings: temples or public buildings, including the Church of the Virgin Mary, which is a contested case. It was said to have been constructed on part of the site of the destroyed Olympicion, which had been built to honour the Emperor Hadrian (117-138) and earned Ephesus its second title of *neokoros* in about 131 A.D.[140] Ekrem Akurgal states that the church was constructed within the walls of something built in the first half of the 2nd century,[141] which was when a temple to Hadrian would have been built. By the mid-5th century such a temple could have safely been disregarded.

Plate 15.3. Church of St Mary. Photo: Matthias Holländer, 2013.

15.6. The Church of the Virgin and the Councils of Ephesus

The church dedicated to the Virgin was built not far beyond the Grand Theatre and the wall of the apse and some columns in the sanctuary have survived (Plate 15.3). It has been assumed that the two Church Councils which were held in Ephesus were held here, but recent excavations have concluded that the Church was not built until after the first of these councils, Ephesus I, which is dated 431/432 A.D.

Although he did not attend it, the first Council of Ephesus was called by the emperor, Theodosius II (401-450) to decide upon the title *Theotokos* (meaning 'God bearer') for the Virgin. The Council also debated the deposition of Patriarch Nestorius, who had not been elected patriarch but appointed by the emperor. Nestorius opposed the term *Theotokos* and held that the nature of Christ was a 'conjunction' of the two natures (God and man) rather than a 'union' of two natures. In 430, he had been condemned and deposed by Pope Celestine (422-432). The First Council of Ephesus confirmed that deposition and Nestorius was exiled to Upper Egypt in 436 A.D. The Council also confirmed the title *Theotokos* for the Virgin, which both reflected and enhanced her emerging cult.[142] This does not imply, however, that Ephesus was deliberately chosen for the Council because of a particular devotion to Mary, although the connection seems logical.

Some years later, in Constantinople, theological turmoil over some finer points of Christology resulted in Pope Leo I's advice being sought. His written reply (or *Tome*) restated old doctrine but a second council at Ephesus, Ephesus II, was called by the same emperor, Theodosius II. In c.448 it excommunicated Pope Leo and refused to have his *Tome* read. Pope Leo called it the 'Robbers' Council' and it is not regarded as valid.[143]

15.7. The House of the Virgin Mary, Near Ephesus

The inside of this house has been converted into a church, based upon a vision received by a German nun, Anna Katherina Emmerich (1774-1824). Following her detailed description, a search was made for Mary's house by Lazarian priests and in 1891 this place was found. It reflects the belief that, after the Crucifixion, the Virgin was taken by St John to live with him in Ephesus where both were buried.

This is a healing place visited by Muslims as well as Christians. In 1967 Pope Paul VI celebrated High Mass here and consecrated Mary's House as a place of prayer and Pope Benedict XV visited it and prayed for peace between peoples because Mary is honoured also by Muslims.[145]

Plate 15. 4. Traditional house of the Virgin, Ephesus.[144]

Due to St Paul's itinerant preaching, Ephesus had a thriving church, which was either founded by St John, or perhaps led by him later. Philip the deacon, of Acts 6:5, lived at nearby Hieropolis (Pamukkale), with probably three of his daughters. He was said to have been a man *"full of the Spirit and of wisdom"* (Acts 6:3) and one of his daughters, Hermione, built a healing clinic for the poor and homeless and guest rooms for travellers, in Ephesus, assisted by her sister, Eukhidia. Hermoine lived to a great age and people came to her from near and far for counsel and to hear her tell about the apostles and the early days of the church. The 2nd century Bishop of Ephesus, Poylcrates, called her one of the "Great Lights" of the Early Church[146] and reported that one of the sisters was buried in Ephesus.[147] Certain saints were buried along the Sacred Way near the Magnesian or eastern Gateway: Timothy, Philip, Barnabas's brother Aristobulus, Paul of Thesbes, and the martyrs Adauctus and Csallisthena, and perhaps also Hermoine.[148]

As noted, there is a strong Christian tradition that Jesus' cousin, John-ben-Zebedee, cared for the Virgin Mary and, in her later years, took her with him to Ephesus, where he led the church for decades after St Paul's martyrdom (although another tradition holds that Mary died in Jerusalem). As Chapter 16 will note, St John's presence in Asia Minor is associated with his exile by Domitian to the Island of Patmos, near Ephesus, but he was released during the short reign of the Emperor Nerva (96-98) - but scholars disagree on whether there was one or two Johns: John the Elder and the Apostle John.

15.8. The Byzantine Church of St John Overlooking Ephesus

An important Byzantine church was built in the 6th century by the Emperor Justinian, over the grave of St John, replacing an earlier church that had a wooden roof. This great church is cruciform in shape with a semi-circular apse. The later roof of this church was topped by six domes. The gave of St John, in the crossing of the nave and transept, is beneath the central dome.

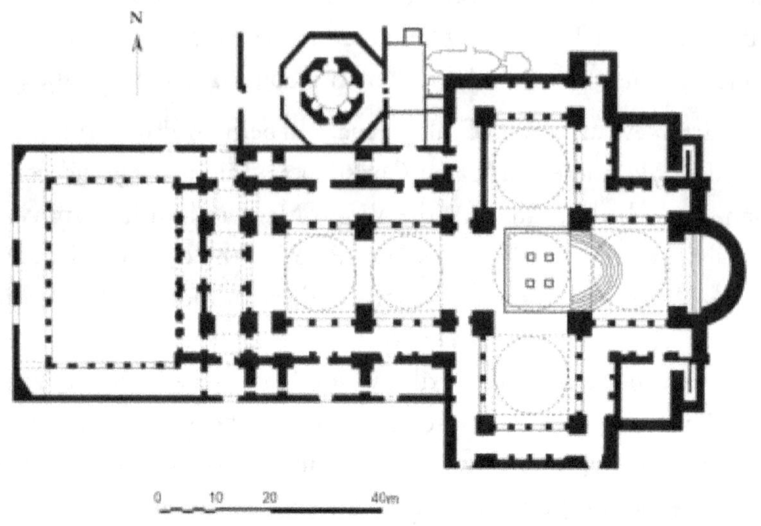

Plate 15.5a. Church of St John on Mt Ayasoluk.[149]

The grave (pictured in Plate 15.5b) was central. As Plate 15.5a shows, the semi-circular *synthronon*, where the clergy sat, faces the gravesite which was protected by a canopy that was supported by four thin pillars. There was a courtyard at the front and later a high wall was built around the church to protect it from Arab attacks. To the North, a separate domed octagonal baptistery with a font, which was decorated with wall-paintings in the 10th century, has recently been excavated.

Plate 15.5b. St John's Church, looking West from the Synthronon.[i]

15.9. The Cave or Grotto of St Paul near Ephesus

A relatively well-preserved wall-painting of St Paul and his protégée, St Thekla, can be found in this grotto. Thekla's tradition was generated in about 160 A.D., according to Tertullian (c.160-c.220) by an apocryphal work called ' *The Acts of Paul and Thekla*.'[150] This was included in the fragmentary text of ' *The Acts of Paul*', a work that was widely read in Antiquity and profoundly influenced both men and women, although Tertullian said that the presbyter (priest) who had written it was dismissed because of his disregard for historical accuracy.[151]

Plate 15. 6th-century wall painting of Paul and Thekla. Public domain.

Generations of Ephesian Christians used the cave or grotto of St Paul as a gathering place and they decorated the walls of its long entrance-corridor with graffiti and paintings. The 6th century paintings of Ss Paul and Thekla were later damaged by an iconoclast who opposed women-in-ministry, to rob St Thekla of her eyesight and her right hand. Paulos and Thekla are both named in Greek. Both were making the sign of blessing. The cave became a place of pilgrimage in the Byzantine Era when it was modified, internally. Pictures and inscriptions were added to it, even up the 11th century.

To summaries Thekla's story: when she first overheard St Paul preach she was transfixed by his teachings and became his disciple. Refusing to marry her fiancé, she became an ascetic and dressed as a man. She travelled around with Paul, baptised herself in a pond of killer seals and was sent out by Paul to evangelise and teach. After miraculously escaping death many times she eventually became a martyr.[152] There may be some fact behind her fascinating but mysterious story but, if so, St Paul gave no hint of her in his canonical epistles. What mattered was that, in Antiquity, everyone believed in her.

Plate 15.7. Thekla's shrine, Turkey. Public domain.

Thekla's example was a challenge to emerging male authority as she was an apostle as well as a teacher and evangelist, which apparently contradicted Paul's canonical teachings. Because her name was not bolstered by any New Testament reference her cult was suppressed by the Western Church but her influence continued in the East. In the 5th and 6th centuries, Thekla's image featured on many flasks and lamps, keepsakes that pilgrims took home from her shrines and monasteries in Syria and Turkey, which still exist.[153] Their wide dispersion demonstrates Thekla's popularity with ordinary people. Thekla's popularity even rivalled that of the Virgin Mary[154] although her very existence is now doubted; except as mythology spiced with exaggerated miracles.

What mattered most about Thekla was not objective 'truth' about her existence but that her tradition was believed, copied and elevated. At this time asceticism was an emerging trend and Gnostic ideas proliferated with a tendency towards renunciation of the material world: food, bathing, sleep, the body, sexuality, recreation and soft bedding. In *The Acts of Paul and Thekla* sexual renunciation was stressed (an element that was even emerging in the church in Ephesus in the Pauline Period, see I Tim. 4:3).

Thekla, a constantly changing metaphor, was a mysterious and unreal figure whose anonymity was her strength as she morphed into other realities as needed.[155] The church had only two options for dealing with unconventional women: they were either suppressed or used in official propaganda. Because the martyr Thekla was non-corporeal she could no longer be imprisoned, suppressed or martyred, so she was elevated as an example for ordinary people to copy, even the poor.

15.10. The Tomb of St Luke in Ephesus

This martyrium, discovered in 1865 and excavated in 1908 and 1997, was built to the East of the State Agora in Ephesus in an old cemetery. It was originally a fountain. It was soon surrounded by many graves as people chose to be buried near so prominent a saint and evangelist who had spent years in the city with St Paul.

It was an octagonal structure. Above, it was surmounted by a drum that supported a dome. It was built in the 2nd century and became a church in the 4th-5th century but it was destroyed in the 7th century. It was rebuilt upon a high podium over a burial crypt which could easily be entered. When it was rebuilt (in the Muslim period) it was beautified with wall-frescoes, mosaic floors and marble decorations and continued to be important to the remaining Christians until the 14th century.[156]

15.11. Cave of the Seven Sleepers near Ephesus

This ruined catacomb complex of caves, tombs, niches and churches on Mt Pion commemorates seven Christian lads who were escaping persecution by the Emperor Decius in the mid 3rd century. They fell asleep here and awoke during the reign of Theodosius II to find that everyone was a Christian.

**Plate 15.8. Cave of the Seven Sleepers,
Mt Pion, Ephesus.[157]**

This site became a place of pilgrimage in the Middle Ages. The details differ in the different sources, and the Quran (18.9.26 [2]) even has a version of the story.[158] This story is a metaphor for the rapid spread of Christianity under Emperor Constantine the Great: one minute believers were being persecuted and when they awoke the whole world had been converted.

15.12. St Paul's Prison in Ephesus

In II Cor. 1:8 St Paul wrote of *"the affliction that came to us in the province of Asia"* but what these afflictions were remains a mystery, filled in by ' *the Acts of Paul'* which says that Paul was shut in prison in irons to await his time in the area with lions; which might well have been true. Today there is a site designated as Paul's prison but it is closed to tourists.

15.13. Conclusions

This assortment of interesting sites in Ephesus illustrates many changes to the city under Christian emperors (in Byzantine times). Most were directly connected to the earliest founders of the church, as Christians often wanted to fill in the blanks where Scripture is silent and some sites became popular even though their narratives are legendary.

This indicates that Christian narratives had seeped into grassroots culture, which is still in evidence when local Muslim people show regard for or veneration of sites such as the House of the Virgin Mary and the Cave of the Seven Sleepers.

Chapter 16
St John and the Island of Patmos

Plate 16.1. Skela on Patmos.
A jewel in the Aegean Sea. Photograph: D. Campbell.

Justin Martyr was the first Christian writer to equate John-son-of-Zebedee with John the Elder who wrote the Biblical *Book of Revelation* (*Dialogue With Trypho*, 81.4) but that is to be expected as there were very few before him. Justin Martyr was born in the Holy Land in about 100 A.D. and became a Jesus-believer in about 130A.D. He then went to Ephesus to teach and that is where he conducted his dialogue with the Jew, Trypho, in c.135 A.D. The said John had only been dead 30 or 40 years as he had died in 95 - 100 A.D. He was still a revered and remembered apostle. Justin Martyr had an excellent opportunity to learn Christian history both in Nablus/Shechem and then in Ephesus where all the older Christians had been eyewitnesses to St John's ministry. Various other ancient sources agree that John, son-of-Zebedee, led the church in Ephesus in his senior years and was buried there.

John himself (Rev. 1:9) and four other sources, including Eusebius, Bishop of Caesarea (*H.E.*, II.17-18), inform us that he was exiled from Ephesus onto the rugged, volcanic Island of Patmos. The other sources are Clement of Alexandria (*What Rich Man Can Be Saved*), Irenaeus (*Against Heresies*, III. 3-4; V.3, 23) and Jerome (*Commentary on Galatians* VI.1).

The small Island of Patmos, which is 55-60 km out to sea, is only 12 km long and about 7km wide. It was not deserted but had been inhabited since 3,000 B.C. Ii is not very fertile, with few large trees, so that the sea has always been the main source of food. Various Roman writers (such as Dio Cassius and Pliny) provide relevant information.

People exiled to Patmos, including to work in the mines there, included criminals, such as robbers, and people who engaged in witchcraft and soothsaying. Inhabitants included government officials, soldiers, merchants, fishermen, fishmongers, dockworkers and the inhabitants of the under-belly of the ancient world's port-cities who mainly lived around the natural harbour (pictured) in a town now called Skela. There were also village people and priests/priestesses of the island's three temples: those of Aphrodite/Venus, Artemis/Diana of the Ephesians and her twin brother, Apollo.

St John was not kept in chains and was free to move about on the island and engage in quiet evangelism. He, himself, said his exile was part of a persecution, which is believed to have occurred towards the end of the reign of the Emperor Domitian (81-96 A.D.). John was freed by the Emperor Nerva whose reign was very short (96-98 A.D.).

John lived on in Ephesus, into the reign of Trajan (98-117) and must have been over 90 years of age when he departed this life as, by the end, he had to be carried into church. A church was erected over his grave site in the 4th century and an even more impressive one replaced it. This church, which was cross-shaped, with six domes, a semi-circular apse and a large walled courtyard, was built by the Byzantine Emperor Justinian (527-565 A.D.) (Plate 15.5a/b).

Because of St John's time there, Patmos has been a tourism hotspot since c.1100, when St Chrystodulus built the Monastery of St John on the highest peak, but in the 1st century the island would have been remote, windswept and perhaps even dangerous because of the criminal element. Even today, during winter, tourism ceases as even large ships often cannot safely dock there. From my experience the winter weather around the Mediterranean has not changed since St Paul was shipwrecked in its waters (Acts 27:1-6). St John was on Patmos for perhaps eighteen months and the locals believe that he lived in a cave or grotto. No wonder he only wrote one circular letter to be shared by all of the congregations under his care especially as getting letters off the island might have been very difficult.

As he was alone, John had time to think about the state of the church and the world and to pray about the future, and his revelations laid the foundation for his unique work, the *Apocalypse of John* (called *Revelations*). It is thought that he witnessed one of the many eruptions of the nearby island of Santorini/Thera, and that it inspired much of the imagery of his *Apocalypse,* but none occurred during his period on Patmos.

Chapter 17
Concluding Remarks

There was a moment in time, between the destruction of Jerusalem in 70 A.D. and the rise of the power of the Papacy in Rome, when Ephesus was the greatest city of Christianity. Many of the greatest Christian personalities were apparently associate with it in the 1st century: St Paul, St Luke, St John, the Virgin Mary, St Timothy and Philip the deacon and his prophetic daughters, only one of whom may have married. Philip's family lived in nearby Hieropolis into the 2nd century and one daughter (known as Hermoine) apparently lived and ministered in Ephesus where either she or her sister (known as Eukhidia) was buried. The memory of these great leaders was kept alive by and within the many Byzantine churches built in their memory, some of which continue to be meaningful as Christians still occasionally celebrate the Eucharist (Holy Communion) within the ruins of the churches of St John and St Mary.

The Ephesian church had strong roots and sound teaching, which is reflected in the esteem indicated in the circular letter that St Paul sent first to the port city (Ephesus) and which is now known as *Epistle to the Ephesians*, and also in the approval recorded in Rev. 2:1-3. After Paul's martyrdom the Christians there worked hard, endured much persecution and doggedly persevered, although lacking the inspiring and motivating power of love they once had experienced.

The army of the Goths invaded the area and destroyed Ephesus in 262/283 A.D., including the Temple of Artemis, which was, however, rebuilt. In 401 A.D., St John Chrysostom (at one time Patriarch of Constantinople) had the Artemision destroyed and today only one solitary column of it remains standing in a swampy field outside the ancient city.[159] Some of its ivory carvings and decorated marble elements are kept in the British Museum and the Istanbul Museum.

In the Byzantine period the city flourished and the many fine churches were built. Eventually a new settlement, Selçuk, was established on the nearby Mount Ayasoluk, within the Castle of Ayasoluk; away from the malarial swamp. The great city of Ephesus was deserted and fell into decay. It was never rebuilt as a port city as the harbour had silted up beyond repair. The remains of the ancient city have been excavated for a century and it is said that excavation and research into the city could continue for another 1,000 years.[160]

The quality of the archaeological remains make Ancient Ephesus a popular tourist destination and excavations can easily continue, assisted by Austrian experts, because the area is no longer inhabited. Unlike other important ancient Christian sites, such as Jerusalem, Athens and Rome, which have been built upon for the 2,000 years since the 1st century, ancient Ephesus was eventually abandoned and never rebuilt so we have both textual evidence and archaeological evidence for it.

The city has cemented a place of affection in the minds of Christians for two millennia because of the place of affection it held in St Paul's mind, although after Paul left Ephesus some Christians came under the influence of Gnosticism (which was falsely called knowledge) (I Tim. 6:20). In comparison with the people of Corinth, however, the Ephesians' Christianity was not flamboyant. Just as their cults had been well organised before the message of Jesus Christ was brought to them they remained committed Christians in the Early Byzantine Period. They gradually accepted Islam but perhaps they had no choice, especially as the Byzantine capital, Constantinople, eventually fell to Muslim forces in the mid-15th century and their Greek language and culture were suppressed; even brutally.

In the 1st century the Ephesians set an example to other churches in hard work and in enduring persecution and suffering (Rev. 2:2f) which remains increasingly relevant in today's world.

Appendix 1

A statue of Hadrian in Ephesus was accompanied by an inscription (| Ephesos II 274) which translates:

"for his unsurpassed gifts to Artemis: he gave the goddess rights over inheritances and deposits and her own laws; he provided shipments of grain from Egypt, he made the harbours navigable and diverted the river Kaystros which silts up the harbour..."

(Price, 1984, 175, cited by Deirdre Hough).

BIBLIOGRAPHY

Primary Sources

Holy Bible, New International Version (London: Hodder and Stoughton, 1978).

'Clement of Rome: Epistle to Corinthians Complete'. https://www.ellopos389-415.[1]net/elpenor/greek-texts/fathers/clement-rome/epistle-corinthians.asp

Eusebius, *History of the Church from Christ to Constantine*, (Andrew Louth (ed.), G. A, Williamson (trans.), Harmondsworth: Penguin, 1965/1990).

Preamble to 'Clement of Rome: Epistle to Corinthians Complete'. https://www.ellopos389-415.[2]net/elpenor/greek-texts/fathers/clement-rome/epistle-corinthians.asp

Jerome, *Commentary on Galatians*

Josephus, *Antiquities of the Jews.*

Lactantius, *On the Deaths of the Persecutors*, (J. L. Creed, trans.) (Oxford: Clarendon Press, 1984).

Louth, Andrew (ed.), *Early Christian Writers*, M. Staniforth, trans., (London: Penguin, 1968/1987).

Strabo, *Geography* 10.3.13.

'The Acts of Paul' including 'The Acts of Paul and Thecla'.

'The Acts of Paul and Thecla', Jeremiah Jones (trans. c.1700), https://www.pbs.org/wgbh/pages/frontline/shows/religion/maps/primary/theclas.html [3]

Reference Works

Boardman John, et al. (eds), *The Oxford History of the Classical World* (Oxford, New York: Oxford University Press, 1986).

---

1.   https://www.ellopos389-415/

2.   https://www.ellopos389-415/

3.   https://www.pbs.org/wgbh/pages/frontline/shows/religion/maps/primary/theclas.html

Cross, F. L. and E. A. Livingstone (eds), *Oxford Dictionary of the Christian Church*

(London: Oxford University Press, 1958/1961, 1972).

Marshall L. H. et al. (eds), *New Bible Dictionary (NBD)* 3rd edition, (Oxford University Press, 1992).

Zondervan Exegetical Commentary on the New Testament vol. 10 (Grand Rapids, 2010).

Secondary Sources

Akurgal, Ekrem, *Ancient Civilizations and Ruins of Turkey,* (Istanbul, 1963).

Alexander, David and Pat (eds.) *The Lion Handbook of the Bible* (Lion Publishing: Oxford, U.K.,1973, 1983).

Bar-Am, Aviva, *Beyond the Walls: Churches of Jerusalem* (Jerusalem: Ahva Press, 1998).

Barnett, Paul, *Jesus & the Rise of Early Christianity* (Inter Varsity Press, 1999).

Bauckham, Richard, *Jesus and the Eyewitnesses: The Gospels as Eyewitness Testimony* 2nd ed. *(Grand Rapids, MI: Eerdmans, 2006/ 2014).*

Boer, Harry R., *A Short History of the Early Church* (Eerdmans, 1976).

Bowersock, G. W., Peter Brown and Oleg Grabar (eds), *Interpreting Late Antiquity* (Belnap Press of Harvard University Press, 1999/2001).

Campbell, Deslee, *Great Christian Women We Have Forgotten* (Shofarot Publications and Amazon, 2020).

Campbell, Deslee, *Why a Roman Emperor Rebuilt Jerusalem and Jerash* (Barnes & Noble, 2023).

Campbell, Justin and Deslee Campbell, *Synagoga's Heritage: Tabernacle, Temple, Synagogue and Church*, (xlibris, 2020).

Chapple, Allan, 'Getting Romans to the Right Romans', *Tyndale Bulletin*, 62.2 (2011).

Cohick, Lynn H. and Amy Brown Hughes, *Christian Women of the Patristic World* (Baker, 2017).

Davis, Stephen J., *The Cult of St Thecla: A Tradition of Women's Piety in Late Antiquity* (Oxford UP, 2001).

Elsner, Jaś, *Imperial Rome and Christian Triumph* (Oxford University Press, 1998).

Foster, John, *After the Apostles* (London, 1951/1961).

Guthrie, Donald, *The Pastoral Epistles* (rev.) (Leicester, U.K., Inter-Varsity Press, 1990).

Hough, Deirdre, 'What can archaeology and history of Ephesus tell us about Paul's ministry there?'

A thesis for Avondale College of Higher Education, 2013.

Jansen, Gemma, 'The Toilets of Ephesus. A Preliminary Report', in *Proceedings of the Twelfth International Congress on the "History of Water Management and Hydraulic Engineering in the Mediterranean Region Ephesus/Selçuk, Turkey, October 2-10, 2004*, Gilbert Wiplinger (ed.), (Peeters, 2006).

Kostenberger, A. J., and T. R. Schreiner (eds), *Women in the Church: an analysis and application of I Timothy 2:9-15* (ed.2) (Grand Rapids, MI, Baker Academic, 2005).

Laden, Jonathan, 'Pompeii Fast-Food Restaurant Uncovered', *Bible History Daily*, December 2020.

LiDonnici, Lynn R., 'The Images of Artemis Ephesia and Greco-Roman Worship: A Reconsideration', Harvard Theological Review *85.4*.

Murphy-O'Connor, Jerome, *St Paul's Ephesus: Texts and Archaeology* (Collegeville, MIN: Liturgical Press, 2008).

Nassar, Mohamad, 'Hadrian's Arches From Roman Period, Jordan: A Comparative Study, Mediterranean Archaeology and Archaeometry, *14.1 (2014)*.

Oden, Thomas C., *How Africa Shaped the Christian Mind: Rediscovering the African Seedbed of Western Christianity* (Downers Grove, IL.: Inter Varsity Press Books, 2007).

Ronny Reich, 'The Hot Bath-House (balneum), the Miqweh and the Jewish Community in the Second Temple Period', Journal of Jewish Studies *39.1 (1988), 102-107.*

Strelan, Rick, *Paul, Artemis and the Jews of Ephesus* (Berlin/New York, 1996).

Swidler, L. and A., *Women Priests* (NY: Paulist Press, 1977).

Tameanko, Marvin, *Monumental Coins: Buildings and Structures on Ancient Coins* (Iola, WI, 1999).

Tenney, Merrill C., *New Testament Times: Understanding the World of the First Century (London: Angus Hudson, 2002/2003).*

Torjesen, Karen Jo, *When Women were Priests* (Harper: San Francisco, 1995).

Trebilco, Paul, *The Early Christians in Ephesus from Paul to Ignatius* (2nd ed.) *(Grand Rapids: Eerdmans, 2007).*

Wand, J. W. C., *A History of the Early Church*, (London: Methuen, 1961).

Wilder, Terry L., 'Phoebe, the Letter-Carrier of Romans, and the Impact of Her Role on Biblical Theology', *Southwestern Journal of Theology*, 56.1. (2013).

Witherington III, Ben, 'Was Paul a Pro-Slavery Chauvinist? Making sense of Paul's seemingly mixed moral messages', *Bible Review* 20.2 (April, 2004).

Electronic Sources

Arnold, Clinton E., 'Ephesians' in *Zondervan Exegetical Commentary*, vol. 10.

https://zondervanacademic.com/blog/who-wrote-ephesians [4]

Arnold, I. R. (1972), 'Festivals of Ephesus', https://www.jstor.org/stable/803607

---

4.   https://zondervanacademic.com/blog/who-wrote-ephesians

Atsma, Aaron J., 'Cybele Cult',
https://www.theoi.com/Cult/CybeleCult.html

Barr, Jane, 'The Vulgate Genesis and St Jerome's Attitude to Women',   https://resources.saylor/www.resource/archived/site/wp-content/uploads/2011/04/The-Vulgate

Berding, Kenneth, 'The Fourth Missionary Journey: What Happened to Paul After Acts?'
The Good Book Blog.
https://biblestudytools.com-bible-study-topical-studies-the-fourth-missionary-journey-what-happened-to-paul-after-acts-html

Booth, Catherine Mumford, 'Female Ministry: or, Woman's Right to Preach the Gospel', published in The Voice, crivoice.org/WT-cbooth.html Baugh, S. M., 'Cult Prostitution in New Testament Ephesus: A Reappraisal', ctsjets.org/files/JETS-PDFs/42/42-3/42-3-pp445-460.JETS.pdf.

Carlson-Ghost, Mark, 'Philip's Daughters, "Great Lights" of the Early Church', markcarlson-ghost.com/index-php/2016/09/17/philips-daughters-prophets-names/

Chapple, Allan, 'Getting Romans to the Right Romans', *Tyndale Bulletin*, 62.2 (2011), 195-214.
www.Tyndale.com.cam.aqc.uk/Tyndale-Bulletin

Campbell, Deslee, *Great Christian Women We Should Remember* (ebook, 2020).

Definbaugh, Bob, 'The Uniqueness of Ephesians Among the Epistles',
https://bible.org/seriespage/1-uniqueness-ephesians-among-epistles [5]

'Excavations in Ephesus',
www.ephesus.co/ephesus-selcuk-excavations.html

Gill, N. S., for ThoughtCo, 'The Thesmophoria',
https://www.thoughtco.org/thesmophoria-111764

---

5.   https://bible.org/seriespage/1-uniqueness-ephesians-among-epistles

Islam, Joseph A., 'The Sleepers of the Cave – The Quran, Historical Sources and Observations',
https://www.quaranmessage.com [6]
Kimmerle, Lurie, 'Goddess Worship and the Apostle Paul', 2017, medium.com/@luriekimmerle/goddess-worship-and-what-st-paul-knew-bdb96db6df3e Knight, Kevin, for *New Advent*,
https://www.newadvent.org/fathers/0103303.htm
Knight, Kevin, for *New Advent*, 'Epistle of Ignatius to the Ephesians', Text https://www.newadent.org/fathers/0104.htm
Mowczko, Marg, 'The prominence of women in the cults of Ephesus', 2014,
https://margmowczko.com/the-prominence-of-women-in-the-cultic-life-of-ephesus [7]
Ovadia, Asher-Sonia Mucznik, 'Apollo and Artemis in the Decapolis', ResearchGate, 3/2019,
https://www.researchgate.net/publication/331651814
Peppiatt, Lucy, 'Wealth in Ancient Ephesus and the First Letter to Timothy: Fresh Insights from Ephesus by Xenophon of Ephesus', cbeinternational.org/resource/book/wealth-ancient-ephesus-and-first-letter-timothy-fresh-insights-ephesiaca
Roberts, Mark D., 'Ancient Ephesus and the New Testament: How our knowledge of the ancient city of Ephesus enriches our knowledge of the New Testament', https://www.patheos.com/blogs/markroberts/series/ancient-ephesus-and-the-new-testament/
Stub, Sara Toth, 'Remembering Hadrian, Destroyer of the Jews', 2016.
www.thetower.org/article/remembering-hadrian-destroyer-of-the-jews [8]
The Bible Journey, 'Paul's 1st Letter to Timothy in Ephesus',

---

6.   http://www.quaranmessage.com/

7.   https://margmowczko.com/the-prominence-of-women-in-the-cultic-life-of-ephesus

8.   http://www.thetower.org/article/remembering-hadrian-destroyer-of-the-jews

https://www.thebiblejourney.org/biblejourney/1/16-pauls-letters-to-timothy

The Ephesus Foundation U.S.A.

https://ephesusfoundationusa.org/projects/tomb-of-st-luke [9]

END NOTES

1. Rick Strelan, *Paul, Artemis and the Jews of Ephesus* (Berlin/New York, 1996); Ekrem Akurgal, *Ancient Civilizations and Ruins of Turkey* (Istanbul, 1983), 156.

2. Paul Trebilco, *The Early Christians in Ephesus from Paul to Ignatius,* 2nd *ed. (Eerdmans, 2007), proposes Pauline, Johannine, Nicolatians and others.*

3. Athens granted Hadrian the titles 'Olympios' in 128/29, 'Panhellenios' and, in 132, 'Panionios', see D. Campbell, *Why a Roman Emperor Rebuilt Jerusalem and Jerash* (2023), 4.4.

4. The Stadium was destroyed by religious fanatics as though to take revenge, Deirdre Hough, 'What can archaeology and history of Ephesus tell us about Paul's ministry there?' Thesis for Avondale College of Higher Education, 2013, (citing Erdemgil et al., 2011, 105).

5. Dating by Akurgal, *op.cit.,* 156; recently contested in 'Excavations in Ephesus',

www.ephesus.co/ephesus/ephesus-selcuk-excavations.html

6. Photograph: D. Campbell.

7. Mohamad Nassar, 'Hadrian's Arches From Roman Period, Jordan: A Comparative Study, *Mediterranean Archaeology and Archaeometry,* 14.1 (2014), 250.

8. Photograph by Nick M. 1982. Public domain.

9. Jaś Elsner, *Imperial Rome and Christian Triumph* (Oxford University Press, 1998), 204.

---

10. Clinton E. Arnold, Ephesians Zondervan Exegetical Commentary on the New Testament vol.10 (Grand Rapids, 2010.), 128f.

11. I. R. Arnold, 'Festivals of Ephesus'

https://www.jstor.org/stable/803607

12. Hough, *op.cit.*, 138, citing Wilson, 2010.

13. *Ibid.*, 101, citing Erdemgil et al., 2000.

14. Lynn R. LiDonnici, 'The Images of Artemis Ephesia and Greco-Roman Worship: A Reconsideration', *Harvard Theological Review* 85.4, f/note 21, citing the German Corpus in 8 volumes.

15. Clinton E. Arnold, *op.cit.*, 128f.

16. Trebilco, *op.cit.*, 22 and Hough, *op.cit.*, 126.

17. Two magical amulets, for example.

18. Hough, *op.cit.*, 37, citing Floyd Filson, 1945, 77 who opined that *"by the late 1st century emperor worship had become quite widespread"*.

19. Marshall et al. (ed), *NBD, s.v.*, Ephesus; says only three times.

20. Marvin Tameanko, *Monumental Coins: Buildings and Structures on Ancient Coins* (Iola, WI, 1999), 33.

21. Hough, *op.cit.*, 14ff, citing Murphy O'Connor and Trebilco.

22. David and Pat Alexander (eds.) *The Lion Handbook of the Bible* (Lion Publishing: Oxford, U.K.,1973, 1983), 620.

23. Disputed by S. M. Baugh, 'Cult Prostitution in New Testament Ephesus: A Reappraisal', *JETS* 42.3, September 1999, 413-460.

ctsjets.org/files/JETS-PDFs/42/42-3/42-3-pp445-460.JETS.pdf.

24. Elsner, *op.cit.* , 204f.

25. *Ibid.*

26. Asher Ovadia and Sonia Mucznik, 'Apollo and Artemis in the Decapolis', *ResearchGate*, March, 2019, 520, online.

27. E.g., Mark D. Roberts, 'Ancient Ephesus and the New Testament: How our knowledge of the ancient city of Ephesus enriches our knowledge of the New Testament',

https://www.patheos.com/blogs/markroberts/series/ancient-ephesus-and-the-new-testament/

28. E.g., Marg Mowczko, 'The prominence of women in the cults of Ephesus', 2014, https://margmowczko.com/the-prominence-of-women-in-the-cultic-life-of-ephesus

29. Campbell, 'Why a Roman Emperor Rebuilt ..', *op.cit.*, 4.4.

30. Strabo, Geography 10.3.13, cited by Aaron J. Atsma, 'Cybele Cult', https://www.theoi.com/Cult/CybeleCult.html

31. Tameanko, *op.cit.*, 27.

32. Akurgal, *op.cit.*, 147-154.

33. Elsner, *op.cit.*, 204; Streland, *op.cit.*, 120.

34. Hough, *op.cit.*, 128 citing Sokolowski (1965) and later authors.

35. Painting by Eustace LeSueur, The Preaching of St Paul at Ephesus', WGA12613.ipg.

36. Trebilco, *op.cit.*, 17.

37. This gate was widened to three entryways and rebuilt by the Emperor Vespasian (69-79 A.D.) and called the Magnesian Gateway because Magnesia was not far away.

38. Tameanko, *op.cit.*, 27f.

39. This model is in the Miniaturk Park, Istanbul. GNU Free Documentation License version 1.2.

40. Hough, *op.cit.*, 141, and Arnold (1972), 22.

41. Arnold (1972), *op.cit.*, 22.

42. Hough, *op.cit.*, 139, citing Erdemgil et al., 1986; Trebilco, 2007.

43. Photograph by Dennis Jarvis. Creative Commons Attribution Share Alike 2.0 License.

44. Eusebius, *E.H.*. III.28 and IV.14 and Irenaeus in Kevin Knight for *New Advent*, from *Ante-Nicene Fathers* Vol. 1. newadvent.org/fathers/0103303.htm

45. Photograph by José Lutz, 2011, used under Creative Commons Attribution 3.0 License.

46. Strelan, *op.cit.*, 170, footnote 68, citing Trudinger, 1988, 291.

47. Hough, *op.cit.*, 97 citing Ladstatter (2007) and Yoncaci (2007)

48. Creative Commons Attribution 2.0 Generic License.

49. Because stone vessels did not contract ritual contamination Jewish priests and Pharisees preferred them and, if found in numbers, they are indicative of Jewish habitation.

50. Trebilco, *op.cit.,* 48, footnote 224, notes: 1 glass flask (with a menorah and other Jewish symbols), 5 lamps with a menorah each and 2 magical amulets with Jewish characteristics and a number of funerary inscriptions, 45-46.

51. Photograph: Dennis Jarvis, 2005. Public domain.

52. From the photographic collection of G. Eric and Edith Malson. Public domain.

53. Photography by Dennis Jarvis, 2005. Used unchanged under Creative Commons Attribution Share Alike 2.0. Generic license. Posted by Flickr and Wikimedia Commons.

54. Hough, *op.cit.*, 64f.

55. *Ibid.*, 84.

56. *Ibid.*, 61.

57. Design Department Shofarot Publications.

58. Dating by Akurgal, *op.cit.*, 169.

59. Hough, *op.cit.*, 65f.

60. *Ibid.*, 18.

61. Photograph by shankar s from Dubai, UAE. Used unchanged under Creative Commons Attribution 2.0 Generic license: from Wikimedia Commons.

62. Xenophon, Hell. ii.4, I am indebted to Deirdre Hough for this referenced.

63. Hough, *op.cit.*, 20, citing Foss, 2010.

64. The name 'Ayasoluk' derives from the fact that St John was buried there.

65. After Domitian's death his memory was officially damned and his temple was hastily rededicated to his father, Vespasian, so that the

city would not lose one of its honours as 'temple warden', Hough, *op.cit.*, 46.

66. Lucy Peppiatt, 'Wealth in Ancient Ephesus and the First Letter to Timothy: Fresh Insights from Ephesus by Xenophon of Ephesus', commenting upon Gary Hoag. Her paper is a 2017 review of Hoag's Ph.D. thesis.

cbeinternational.org/resource/book/wealth-ancient-ephesus-and-first-letter-timothy-fresh-insights-ephesiaca

67. This file is licensed under the Creative Commons Attribution Share Alike 2.0 Generic License.

68. Hough, *op.cit.*, 61.

69. Gemma Jansen, 'The Toilets of Ephesus. A Preliminary Report', in *Proceedings of the Twelfth International Congress on the "History of Water Management and Hydraulic Engineering in the Mediterranean Region Ephesus/Selçuk, Turkey, October 2-10, 2004*, Gilbert Wiplinger (ed.), (Peeters, 2006), Fig. 2, p. 96. My thanks to Dr Jansen for provision of this article.

70. Used under the terms of GNU Free Documentation License, Version 1.2.

71. A triclinium was a room containing a Roman style divan with three sides, or three divans for up to nine men to recline upon while dining. Women did not recline.

72. Recently, a take-away food outlet was found in the new excavations of 1st century Pompeii, Jonathan Laden, 'Pompeii Fast-Food Restaurant Uncovered', *Bible History Daily*, December 2020.

73. Akurgal, *op.cit.* , 379-382.

74. Photograph by Ronan Reinart. This file is licensed under the Creative Commons Attribution Share Alike 3.0 Unported License.

75. Jesus' disciple, Joanna, was the wife of Herod's steward; Sergius Paulus, a convert, was pro-consul of Cyprus; Dionysius, a convert in Athens, was a political leader; St Ignatius greeted the governor of

Smyrna's wife, children and household (c.107A.D.) and the Emperor Diocletian's wife and daughter were baptised.

76. Marshall et al. (eds), *NBD, op.cit., s.v.* Paul.

77. Eusebius, *H.E.*, II. 23.1 and Josephus *Ant.* XX. 9. 1.

78. Eusebius, *H.E.* II. 25.1ff.

79. E.g., D. Guthrie in L. H. Marshall et al. (eds), *New Bible Dictionary (NBD)* 3rd edition, (Oxford University Press, 1992); F.L. Cross and E.A. Livingstone (eds), *Oxford Dictionary of the Christian Church (ODCC), s.v.* St Paul; Paul Barnett, *Jesus and the Rise of Early Christianity* (Inter Varsity Press, 1999), 341ff.

80. Kenneth Berding, 'The Fourth Missionary Journey: What Happened to Paul After Acts?' The Good Book Blog. https://biblestudytools.com-bible-study-topical-studies-the-fourth-missionary-journey-what-happened-to-paul-after-acts-html

81. *Ibid.*

82. Preamble to 'Clement of Rome: Epistle to Corinthians Complete'.

https://www.ellopos389-415.[10]net/elpenor/greek-texts/fathers/clement-rome/epistle-corinthians.asp

83. See Eusebius, *H.E.* II. 25.1ff.

84. Marshall et al. (eds), *NBD, s.v.,* Luke.

85. The Bible Journey, 'Paul's 1st Letter to Timothy in Ephesus',

https://www.thebiblejourney.org/biblejourney   [11]1/16-pauls-letters-to-timothy

86. Strelan, *op.cit.,* 123.

87. Merrill C. Tenney, *New Testament Times: Understanding the World of the First Century* (London: Angus Hudson, 2002/2003) argues for this option, 261-265.

88. Aviva Bar-Am, *Beyond the Walls: Churches of Jerusalem* (Jerusalem: Ahva Press, 1998), 50-53.

---

10.   https://www.ellopos389-415/

11.   https://www.theboblejourney.org/biblejourney

89. For Mark as Peter's scribe, Papias Bishop of Hierapolis cited by Eusebius *H.E.* III.39.14. Paul Barnett, *Jesus & the Rise of Early Christianity* (Inter Varsity Press, 1999), 392. Richard Bauckham argues that the two collaborated on it, in *Jesus and the Eyewitnesses: The Gospels as Eyewitness Testimony* 2nd ed. (Grand Rapids, MI: Eerdmans, 2006/2014).

90. Thomas C. Oden, *How Africa Shaped the Christian Mind: Rediscovering the African Seedbed of Western Christianity* (Downers Grove, IL.: Inter Varsity Press Books, 2007), 18, 158 and Map 4, on page 40.

91. Lactantius, *On the Deaths of the Persecutors*, (J. L. Creed, trans.) (Oxford: Clarendon Press, 1984), II.

92. See translation of the text by Kevin Knight for New Advent, online.

93. Marshall et al. (ed), *NBD, s.v.* , Onesimus.

94. Terry L. Wilder, 'Phoebe, the Letter-Carrier of Romans, and the Impact of Her Role on Biblical Theology', *Southwestern Journal of Theology*, 56.1. (2013), 44-45.

95. Allan Chapple, 'Getting Romans to the Right Romans', *Tyndale Bulletin*, 62.2 (2011), 213, f/n. 77.

96. Elizabeth Schüssler Fiorenza, 'The Apostleship of Women in Early Christianity, in L. and A. Swidler, *Women Priests* (NY: Paulist Press, 1977), 17.

97. Donald Guthrie, *The Pastoral Epistles* (rev.) (Leicester, U.K., Inter-Varsity Press, 1990), 184.

98. Strelan, *op.cit.,* 119.

99. Marshall et al., *NBD, s.v.* Gaius.

100. Bob Definbaugh, 'The Uniqueness of Ephesians Among the Epistles', https://bible.org/seriespage/1-uniqueness-ephesians-among-epistles

101. The 'agape meal' is argued in Justin Campbell and Deslee Campbell, *Synagoga's Heritage: Tabernacle, Temple, Synagogue and Church*', (xlibris, 2020), Chapter 18.

102. This image by Carole Raddato, 2015, is used under the Creative Commons Attribution Share Alike 2.0 License.

103. The Roman Empire changed hands six times in three decades. Vespasian (69-79) was succeeded by his son Titus (79-81) and another son, Domitian (81-96). Nerva, who was old, was elected by the Senate but had a short reign (96-98). Nerva was said to have adopted Trajan (98-117) who became his heir.

104. Elsner, *op.cit.*, 123.

105. Sara Toth Stub, 'Remembering Hadrian, Destroyer of the Jews', 2016.

www.thetower.org/article/remembering-hadrian-destroyer-of-the-jews[12]

106. Clinton E. Arnold, *op.cit.*, 22.

107. 'Excavations in Ephesus', www.ephesus.co/ephesus-selcuk-excavations.html

108. Jane Barr, 'The Vulgate Genesis and St Jerome's Attitude to Women', citing David Wiesen, *St Jerome the Satirist*,

https://resources.saylor.org/www.resources/archived/site/wp-content/uploads/2011/04/The-Vulgate-Genesis-pdf

109. Christians apparently destroyed the Stadium as an act of revenge.

110. Definbaugh, *op.cit.*, online.

111. *Ibid.*

112. This was a Gnostic sect which either syncretised with paganism or had lax sexual practices.

113. Jerome, *Commentary on Galatians*, VI.10.

114. Strelan, *op.cit.*, 119.

---

115. Karen Jo Torjesen, *When Women were Priests* (Harper: San Francisco, 1995), 33.

116. Marshall et al. (eds), *NBD, s.v.* Eudoia, citing Lightfoot.

117. S. M. Baugh,' A Foreign World: Ephesus in the First Century, in A. J. Kostenberger and T. R. Schreiner (eds), *Women in the Church: an analysis and application of I Timothy 2:9-15* (ed.2) (Grand Rapids, MI, Baker Academic, 2005), 28 cited by Mowczko, *op.cit.*, online.

118. Hough, *op.cit.*, 138, citing Rogers, 1994.

119. Mowczko, *op.cit.,* online.

120. N. S. Gill for ThoughtCo, 'The Thesmophoria', https://www.thoughtco.org/thesmophoria-111764

121. Strelan, *op.cit.*, p. 121.

122. John Boardman et al. (eds), *The Oxford History of the Classical World*, 270.

123. Aaron J. Atsma, 'Cybele Cult', https://www.theoi.com/Cult/CybeleCult.html citing a 5th century Greek lyric by the poet, Pindar.

124. Peppiatt, *op.cit.*, online.

125. Lurie Kimmerle, 'Goddess Worship and the Apostle Paul', 2017, medium.com/@luriekimmerle/goddess-worship-and-what-st-paul-knew-bdb96db6df3e

126. Photograph: Marie Lan Gnguven, 2007. Public domain. The marble portrait is in the Louvre.

127 Ben Witherington III, 'Was Paul a Pro-Slavery Chauvinist? Making sense of Paul's seemingly mixed moral messages,' *BR* 20.2 (April, 2004).

128. Akurgal, *op.cit.*, 154f.

129. *Ibid.*, 168f.

130. *Ibid.*

131. 'The Acts of Paul and Thecla' are part of 'The Acts of Paul'.

132. Published in A. Louth (ed.), *Early Christian Writers*, M. Staniforth, trans (London: Penguin, 1968/1987) and online by Kevin Knight for New Advent.

133. Translation of the text, see Kevin Knight for New Advent, online.

134. Peppiatt, *op.cit.*, online quoting Hoag's thesis.

135. Catherine Mumford Booth, 'Female Ministry: or, Woman's Right to Preach the Gospel', published in The Voice, crivoice.org/WT-cbooth.html

136. For Margaret Fell Fox see Deslee Campbell, *Great Christian Women We Should Remember* (ebook, 2020).

137 Ronny Reich, 'The Hot Bath-House (balneum), the Miqweh and the Jewish Community in the Second Temple Period', Journal of Jewish Studies 39.1 (1988), 102-107.

138. Photograph by Bernard Gragnon, This file is licensed under the Creative Commons Attribution Share Alike 3.0 Unported License.

139. Rudolf Heberdey, c. 1930. Public domain.

140. Béatrice Caserau, 'Sacred Landscapes', in G. W. Bowersock, Peter Brown and Oleg Grabar (eds), *Interpreting Late Antiquity* (Belnap Press of Harvard University Press, 1999/2001), 38f.

141. Akurgal, *op.cit.*, 156.

142. *ODCC, op.cit., s.v.* Nestorianism

143. Harry R. Boer, *A Short History of the Early Church* (Eerdmans, 1976), 178; J. W. C. Wand, *A History of the Early Church*, (London: Methuen, 1961), 240.

144. Photo by Erik Cleves Kristensen .This file is licensed under the Creative Commons Attribution 2.9 Generic license.

145. Roberts, *op.cit.*, online.

146. Torjesen, *op.cit* , 43f; Mark Carlson-Ghost, 'Philip's Daughters, "Great Lights" of the Early Church,' markcarlson-ghost.com/index-php/2016/09/17/philips-daughters-prophets-names/

147. Torjesen, *op.cit.*, 43.

148. Hough, *op.cit.*, 14, 20 citing Foss.

149. Photograph: Maisyas 2008. This file is licensed under the Creative Commons Attribution 3.0 Unported.

150. Jeremiah Jones (trans. c.1700), 'The Acts of Paul and Thecla' https://www.pbs.org/wgbh/pages/frontline/shows/religion/ maps/primary/theclas.html [13]

151. Cross and Livingstone (eds.), *ODCC, op.cit., s.v.,* Acts of Paul 95

152. Lynn H. Cohick and Amy Brown Hughes, *Christian Women of the Patristic World* (Baker, 2017), 10ff.

153. *Ibid., Christian Women* includes three examples: a circular wall-plaque (Fig. 1.2), an ivory panel (one of a series about Thekla) (Fig. 1.3) and a wall-painting in a cave (Fig. 1.1).

154. Stephen J. Davis, *The Cult of St Thecla: A Tradition of Women's Piety in Late Antiquity* (Oxford UP, 2001), 4.

155/i. Photograph: Reinhard G. Jena, 2013, public domain.

155. Cohick and Hughes, *op.cit.,* 24f.

156.   The   Ephesus   Foundation   U.S.   A. https://ephesusfoundationusa.org/projects/tomb-of-[14] st-luke [15]

157. CNU Free Documentation License Version 1.2.

158. Joseph A. Islam, 'The Sleepers of the Cave – The Quran, Historical Sources and Observations',www.quaranmessage.com

159. Tameanko, *op.cit.,* 33.

160. 'Excavations in Ephesus', *op.cit.,* online.

161. Jesus' disciple, Joanna, was the wife of Herod's steward; Sergius Paulus, a convert, was proconsul of Cyprus; Dionysius, a convert in Athens, was a political leader; St Ignatius greeted the governor of Smyrna's wife, children and household (c.111). The Emperor Diocletian's wife and daughter were punished for being

---

13.   https://www.pbs.org/wgbh/pages/frontline/shows/religion/maps/primary/theclas.html

14.   https://ephesusfoundationusa.org/projects/tomb-of-st-luke

15.   https://ephesusfoundationusa.org/projects/tomb-of-st-luke

baptised and his niece was exiled and her husband was martyred as a Christian, John Foster, *After the Apostles* (London, 1951/1961), 43.

Don't miss out!

Visit the website below and you can sign up to receive emails whenever Deslee Campbell publishes a new book. There's no charge and no obligation.

https://books2read.com/r/B-A-LSULB-LJKJF

BOOKS2READ

Connecting independent readers to independent writers.

Also by Deslee Campbell

Memorable Christians
Phoebe's Sister's: Women Leaders in Early Christianity
Phoebe's Sisters: Women Leaders in Early Christianity
Phoebe's Sisters : Women Leaders in Early Christianity
Bright Shining Lights of an Earlier Era
Shining Lights of the Reformation
Shining Lights of the Reformation
Remarkable Post-Reformation Christians
Remarkable Post-Reformation Christians
Remarkable Post-Reformation Christians
Modern Christian Martyrs
Modern Christian Martyrs
Modern Christian Martyrs
Modern Christian Martyrs ready.doc
Christian Women We Should Remember
Great Christian Men We Have Forgotten
Great Christian Men We Have Forgotten
Great Christian Men We Have Forgotten
Christian Women Leaders of the 20th Century

Shoah Series
Confronting Holocaust Denial

Watch for more at www.synagogueandchurch.com.

About the Author

About the Author

Dr Deslee Campbell, a retired educational psychologist and teacher, is a prolific writer of both fiction and works concerned with history, religion and archaeology. She is particularly interested in art, artefacts and architecture as pathways towards understanding the past. Her doctoral thesis from the University of Sydney is entitled "The Iconography of Women: A Study of Byzantium and the Byzantine-influenced Mediterranean, A.D. 395-1204."

Read more at https://www.youtube.com/@synagogueandchurch911.

www.ingramcontent.com/pod-product-compliance
Lightning Source LLC
Chambersburg PA
CBHW071618150726
48000CB00004B/1776